GHOST
STORIES
OF THE
ROCKY
MOUNTAINS

BARBARA SMITH

LONE
PINE

© 1999 by Barbara Smith and Lone Pine Publishing
First printed in 1999   10 9 8 7 6 5 4
Printed in Canada

The Publisher: Lone Pine Publishing

10145-81 Avenue	202A 1110 Seymour Street	1901 Raymond Ave., SW, Suite C
Edmonton, AB T6E 1W9	Vancouver, BC V6B 3N3	Renton, WA 98055
Canada	Canada	USA

Lone Pine Publishing web site: http://www.lonepinepublishing.com

Canadian Cataloguing in Publication Data
Smith, Barbara, 1947-
  Ghost stories of the Rocky Mountains

  Includes bibliographical references.
  ISBN 1-55105-165-6

  1. Ghosts—Rocky Mountains. 2. Legends—Rocky Mountains. I. Title.
GR580.S665 1999   398.2'097805   C99-910174-9

10/02   985

Editorial Director: Nancy Foulds
Production Manager: David Dodge
Editorial: Nancy Foulds, Volker Bodegom, Erin McCloskey
Layout & Production: Volker Bodegom
Book Design: Michelle Bynoe
Cover Photos: 1880s train, courtesy Kelowna Centennial Museum Association; Castle Mountain, courtesy Mark and Leslie Degner; old building in Bannack, MT, courtesy Dolores Steele; woman's image, courtesy the author
Cover Illustration: Rob Weidemann
Scanning: Chris Taylor, Volker Bodegom
Code: 06
Photos Courtesy of: Robert Smith, except Dolores Steele (pp. 45, 68, 114, 123, 209); Western Mining and Railroad Museum (p. 53); Molly Brown House and Synergy Photo/Graphics (pp. 70, 74); Provincial Archives of Alberta (pp. 115, 117); B.C. Archives, Province of B.C. (p. 121); Flickinger family (pp. 129, 152, 154, 156); Utah State Historical Society (pp. 173, 216).

The publisher gratefully acknowledges the support of the Department of Canadian Heritage.

Dedication

This book is dedicated to my daughter—and dear friend—Deborah, in celebration of the day that we spent *inside* the mountain.

For my grandsons and their peers—who will need forests as much as books—arrangements have been made to plant trees to compensate for those used in publishing this volume.

Contents

Chapter 5: Ghostly Ghost Towns

Chapter 6: The Spirit's Inn

Chapter 7: Ghosts in Public

Chapter 8: Stage Fright

Acknowledgments

Collecting and compiling the stories for this book would not have been nearly as much fun without help from the following people.

Paranormal specialist W. Ritchie Benedict of Calgary continued (as with previous projects) to demonstrate both his amazing research abilities and his generosity by turning up some wonderfully obscure Rocky Mountain-area ghost stories. Thank you, Ritchie.

Arlene Flickinger of Cardston, Alberta, kindly discussed the ghost at Cobblestone Manor with me at length and then followed up by supplying photos to run with the story. Author James Musson of Brightest Pebble Publishing Company, Edmonton, devoted the better part of an evening to my telephone call. Lori Perez of the Western Mining & Railroad Museum in Helper, Utah, responded to my request by supplying some intriguing local history—including a ghost story. Elizabeth Owen Walker, curator at the Molly Brown House Museum in Denver, was most forthcoming in response to my letter of inquiry. Su Richards from the Utah State Historical Society sent along a photograph and a brief history of the haunted building where she works. Dr. Barrie Robinson offered valuable editorial guidance. My husband, Bob Smith, was endlessly helpful to me in the acquisition of photographs. Photographer Dolores Steele was both extremely generous and helpful. As always, I have relied heavily on the services and expertise of the staff of Edmonton Public Libraries, especially the Inter-library Loan Department. Thank you, both for your help and the consistently pleasant way in which it was offered.

There would have been little point, however, in my even attempting to write this book if it weren't for publisher Shane Kennedy and the staff at Lone Pine Publishing whose cheerful and efficient support I've come to rely on. Your efforts on my behalf are extraordinary and deeply appreciated. Thank you, one and all.

Introduction

The enormity and grandeur that we know as the Rocky Mountains began more than a billion years ago as layers of sediment on an ancient seabed. These horizontal strata lay undisturbed until forces deep within the earth's core began shifting and disrupting them, causing the sheets to become nearly vertical. When they finally cracked through the earth's crust, these early mountains looked very different than the Rockies that we see today, for the ice ages still had not sculpted their peaks and valleys.

The Rocky Mountains as we known them are actually made up of approximately one hundred separate mountain ranges that run a distance of some 3000 miles (4800 kilometers), from northern Alberta and British Columbia in Canada, through Montana and Idaho, Wyoming, Utah and Colorado, south to New Mexico in the United States. The mountainous terrain is in places 300 miles (480 kilometers) wide, and some peaks reach elevations of more than 14,000 feet (4300 meters). Such cold geographic facts belie the significance of the mountains to human history, for the breathtaking beauty of the slopes has created a dichotomy—these craggy giants simultaneously beckon yet repel all who approach them.

It is thought that early human arrival at the base of the steep slopes roughly coincided with the end of the last ice age. No doubt the first mystical, magical story about the Rocky Mountains was told soon afterward, and by now a rich heritage of legends has created a wealth of fascinating tales. Ghosts and haunted places are one common theme throughout those mountain stories, and they are the focus of this book.

I'm frequently asked "What is a ghost?" and I'm sure that people asking the question expect that I will have a ready answer for them. I sincerely wish that I did. Some of the world's greatest minds have spent years pondering this subject without coming to any conclusions. As I do not regard myself as any sort of an expert, but only as a collector of folklore, I feel no embarrassment at my lack of a stock answer.

In the context of the thousands of ghost stories that I've been told, some theories explaining the existence of ghosts and haunted places do make more sense than others. For instance, Frederic Myers, one of the founding members of the old and honorable Society for Psychical Research in England, suggested in his book *Human Personality and Its Survival of Bodily Death* (1903) that a ghost is "an indication that some kind of force is being exercised after death" and that this force "is in some way connected with a person" now deceased.

Most other explanations are somewhat of a variation on Myers's proposition. "Leftover energy" (physical or emotional) is a term used to describe the phenomenon that is a ghost. The "psychic imprint" theory holds that the essence of a person has been somehow stamped on the environment in which that person lived. The deceased person's soul has effectively left an imprint on the physical world.

Another theory holds that ghosts are disembodied souls (or energies, or personalities, or spirits) that are usually detectable only by our nearly atrophied sixth sense. Rather than perceiving this otherworldly sensation with our familiar five senses, we notice the hair on our arms or the back of our necks standing up on end, or a tingling sensation on our skin, or the feeling that we are being watched when we know that we are alone.

Other students of the subject support the hypothesis that ghosts are deceased persons whose beings either don't know that they are dead or can't accept death because they feel obligated to complete unfinished business among the living.

Throughout all of these suppositions is the underlying question as to whether a ghost originates with the living person who is experiencing the encounter, or with the ghost itself. Perhaps that point is debatable, but because many people report seeing or sensing the same spirit either at the same time or at different times, the event is certainly more objective than merely a figment of "the mind's eye."

The most strikingly different of all the theses is that of "retrocognition"—seeing or sensing the past. An excellent example of this phenomenon is included in Chapter 7 (see "A Never-ending Battle," p. 182): a husband and wife visiting the Little Bighorn Battlefield National Monument witnessed a vision of a scene that existed during some point in the battle of Custer's Last Stand.

Another concept of a ghost is almost the opposite of retrocognition—sightings of "forerunners" have led people to predict future events. Undeniably some ghosts, such as forerunners, have messages for us, but others just seem to be continuing on about their business oblivious to the world of the living that surrounds them.

Not all ghosts present themselves visually in the shape of humans. Although apparitions and poltergeists fall under the broad definition of the general term "ghost," they have some additional qualities. An "apparition" is a visible presence; it has a discernible physical form. While this form tends to be the popular conception of a ghost, a sighting of an apparition is actually a statistical rarity.

A "poltergeist" is an equally rare type of spectral being that can be identified by its noisy and possibly violent behaviors. It will often move objects and can actually wreak havoc on its surrounding physical environment. Poltergeists are strongly associated with people rather than places. They have been known to follow people for years, even through a succession of moves. In one case that I'm familiar with, a woman's long-standing spirit companion followed her from North America to the British Isles.

A ghost may be present only in the form of a sensation—a person feels that he or she is not alone, although no one else is physically present. Ghosts can also manifest as smells—both pleasant and unpleasant. Other manifestations include ghostly lights and phantom music.

Despite the lack of agreement about what a ghost might be, ghosts exist in all cultures and have been noted throughout history. My own experience in collecting ghost stories has taught me one other consistency: a paranormal encounter is a deeply moving experience. I have yet to have a story told to me in a flippant or even matter-of-fact way. Experiencing a ghost is clearly a profoundly moving occurrence in a person's life. Out of respect for this emotional factor, I have agreed to protect contributors' anonymity when they have requested that I do so.

Some people are much more likely than others to encounter a ghost. I have heard the suggestion that some of us are more attuned to the "wavelength" on which ghosts transmit. Although this sensitivity seems to be naturally occurring, it is also apparent that the ability can either be enhanced with practice or left to diminish.

Being haunted is not necessarily a permanent status for either a person or place. A place that is currently haunted may not always be so. Conversely, just because your home and workplace are ghost-free zones today doesn't mean that they will always be so.

Some ghosts are incredibly tenacious. The ghosts of Roman soldiers are still occasionally spotted roaming the English countryside where they battled two thousand years ago. The phantoms in these reports, though, are old compared to most seen in our times. As I have never heard or read of any place or person being haunted by the ghost of a prehistoric cave dweller, I presume that, like all forms of energy, ghosts eventually weaken to the point of virtual dissipation.

If a place is haunted or if a ghost is present, predictable and distinguishable changes will usually be noted. These changes could include a dramatic temperature drop, either very localized or in a larger area. Apparently sourceless drafts, odors or noises can also indicate a ghostly presence.

An issue of semantics arises in the retelling of ghost stories. There are few true synonyms in the English language, but I have chosen to use the following words interchangeably: specter, spirit, entity, presence, phantom, vision, image, shade, apparition, wraith, manifestation and ghost. (I was once informed that the term "ghost" is an inherently insulting one. I hope that that is not so, because I mean no offence when I use the term.)

The ghost stories found in this book are not works of fiction. As a result, they tend to be somewhat ragged. A fictional account of a haunting will have a nicely structured and highly satisfying presentation—a beginning, a middle and an end. The anecdotes recorded here refuse to be that tidy—they are often merely fragments, which can be somewhat frustrating in a world so fond of neatness. We like to have any loose ends bound up by a story's last sentence—it's more satisfying that way. The stories here, however, are reports of real events, and we all know that life, as we live it, is anything but neat and tidy. I consider myself to be merely a recorder of events and so I have resisted the temptation to recraft any of the stories in order to make them conform to an expected standard. A few people, after reading any of my first four books of true ghost stories, have told me that they find this approach frustrating. I can certainly sympathize, but by now I tend to view the parts of the puzzle that are missing as being as provocative as those that are at hand.

Of course, I'm often asked if I've ever seen a ghost. The intent is, perhaps, to discover if I am following that well-established rule of writing about what I know. The short answer is "no." I'm afraid that in the field of the paranormal I have few firsthand qualifications. It is merely my love of social history, and a lifelong fascination with the possibility that ghosts might exist, that brought me to research and write my books.

If you want a more exotic answer, or perhaps a more exotically qualified author, I offer the following anecdotes. While writing my first book of ghost stories, small objects, always connected with the manuscript or my attempts to complete it, would inexplicably go missing. One day my reading glasses were not where they should have been. I spent nearly an hour searching around the house for them. Finally, in frustration, I gave up the hunt and began to work at the computer without my glasses on. Predictably, a headache caused by eyestrain cut my session short. In order to give my eyes the break that they needed and make myself feel better, I took my dog out for a walk. When I returned, something made me check my briefcase. No one had been in or out of the house in my absence, and to this day I deny having put my glasses in there. Nonetheless, there they were.

Notes from a long-distance telephone interview were the next thing to go missing. I tore the house apart looking for the notepad that I'd written them on, even though I distinctly remembered putting it away in the desk I was at while talking on the phone.

That evening I explained my dilemma to my husband, who presumed that, in my panic to find the notes, I'd not done an organized search. Drawer by drawer, he systematically took everything out of the desk. The steno pad was simply not there. I had no choice but to make the phone call a second time.

Shortly after that second call, I also visited the site in question and soon had plenty of information to write that particular ghost story. Those notes from the original interview had, by then, completely lost their importance. Upon returning home, I opened the desk drawer and the missing notepad was the first thing that I saw.

To say that I was surprised by the discovery would be a major understatement. That night, when I told my husband of my find, all that he could say of the mysteriously disappearing and reappearing notebook was, "It certainly wasn't there when I looked for it."

Some months after that incident, I was preparing to deliver a substantial portion of the manuscript to the publisher. I had set aside the entire day to do nothing but finalize my completed ghost stories. By 11:30 AM I'd already stopped working and went upstairs to the kitchen to make myself some lunch. I wasn't really hungry but I was extremely cold.

Twenty minutes later I was more comfortable and went back downstairs to resume work. I'd barely gotten restarted when, once again, I became cold. Rather than stop again, I simply put a sweatshirt over the long-sleeved T-shirt that I was already wearing. The extra clothes did help, but my concentration was soon affected by my cold hands and feet.

There wasn't much that I could do about my nearly numb fingers; I needed them to type. But I did put on a pair of woolen work socks over my regular socks, and resumed working. Several hours, and a great deal of work later, I turned off my computer. Minutes later, my younger daughter drove up. She was wearing shorts, a sleeveless T-shirt and asking for a cold drink. I still had not warmed up enough to take off any of my extra clothes. We made quite a pair standing there, staring at each other. It was clear that my daughter was the one who was dressed for the weather: the forecasters had predicted a high of 84°F (29°C) and it had certainly reached that.

To explain myself and my strange attire, I asked my daughter to come down to my office with me. Admittedly, a basement is usually cooler than the rest of a house, but what we discovered went way too far. My office was next to the recreation room and I'd been working with the office door open. The recreation room was its usual cool space, but as soon as we stepped through the doorway into the office we could feel a dramatic drop in temperature. We stepped back and forth over the threshold several times, fascinated with the phenomenon.

Feeling decidedly strange about staying in the house under such conditions, we went to our favorite coffee shop. When we returned, the temperature of the office was identical to that of the rest of the basement. Thankfully, whatever negative energy I'd attracted that day has left and never returned.

There was one possibly paranormal event that did occur frequently in that house. No one in our household smokes and yet periodically we smelled cigarette smoke wafting through the place. The first few times that it happened we would search the whole house thoroughly—not to find the smoking ghost but to make sure that there wasn't a fire somewhere. Despite dozens of searches, nothing ever turned up. Eventually we realized that this phenomenon had begun to happen only after my first book of ghost stories had been released. There is a story in that book about our next door neighbor's house being haunted by the owner's late husband, a man named Bill.

Once my husband and I became used to the experience, we decided, somewhat arbitrarily, that it was Bill's spirit that we were detecting when we smelled cigarettes. We were very happy with that conclusion. We no longer had to look for nonexistent fires in the house and we knew that Bill's spirit was very protective of his widow and her house. We presumed that he was a positive, if fleeting, addition to our household. We lived happily with that assumption for years. When we noticed that rather unpleasant odor, we'd just smile at one another and calmly announce "Bill's here again."

That solution to the mysterious smoky smell worked well until I mentioned it to my neighbor, Bill's widow. Unfortunately, she knocked the comfort completely out of our theory with one short sentence—"Bill never smoked." There we were, back at square one, having absolutely no idea why our house would, at times, smell strongly of cigarette smoke. Obviously I believe in the concept of ghosts, and I did make some optimistic guesses about our invisible smoker's identity, but we were never again sure. We eventually moved from that house and, given that the presence did not move with us, those presumptions were probably as incorrect as the original one.

My "closest encounter" with a ghost took place in a restaurant not far from my home. One day I was waiting for a friend to join me for an annual luncheon celebration. It's become traditional to hold this yearly ritual at La Boheme, a restaurant in a charming old east-end building in Edmonton. People had told me that they thought that there might be a presence in the restaurant, and I was hoping to get a chance to ask the owner whether he thought that a ghost was associated with his establishment.

I arrived a bit earlier than our planned meeting time and the restaurant's owner showed me to a quiet table and offered me a cup of coffee while I waited. I decided to take advantage of what I knew would be only a temporary lull. As the man poured my coffee, I mustered up what I hoped was a casual-sounding voice and said, "This building's really old, isn't it? Would you happen to know if it might be haunted?"

The words were no sooner out of my mouth when the lid of the sugar bowl at my table rose up and set itself down beside the bowl. I was grateful that the restaurateur was still beside me and so had also seen the strange movement. At least I knew that if I was seeing things, I wasn't alone in what I was seeing. We both realized that my question had been answered on his behalf, by the spirit herself.

After exchanging incredulous looks, followed by somewhat unnerved smiles, we continued our attempt at conversation.

"Oh, yes," he confirmed, somewhat unnecessarily now. "She usually only comes out late at night, though, after closing."

Those four completely isolated incidents are the closest that I've ever come to the paranormal and, despite the content of the books that I write, I've never encountered anything more dramatic than those events.

This collection is not an attempt to alter your personal belief systems with my convictions or explanations. My intent is merely to entertain and possibly provoke thought in areas that you might not otherwise explore. I do not pretend to be an educator but, if reading this book introduces you to facets of Rocky Mountain history or geography with which you were previously unfamiliar, then I am pleased.

With just a few exceptions, as you'll see, I have purposely excluded mention of the many Native peoples' tales of spirits and the supernatural from this collection. Although these stories would definitely make a fascinating book, I am not qualified to write them.

If anyone knows of other ghostly stories from the Rocky Mountains, I would be delighted to learn of them. You may write to me care of Lone Pine Publishing. In the meantime, I do hope that you enjoy this collection.

Chapter 1

HIGHWAYS AND BYWAYS

By definition, the very existence of the Rocky Mountains presents a formidable barrier to travel. Even on today's well-designed roadways, in the comfort and security of our modern vehicles, the act of getting from one side of the mountains to the other remains, at best, a challenging experience; at worst, it can be a fatal one.

Enormous amounts of energy have been expended in the human endeavor to do the impossible—conquer these geological giants. The resulting human drama has left the atmosphere on and around Rocky Mountain highways and byways severely scarred or, in a word, haunted.

Phantom Hitchhikers

For well over a century, tales of vanishing hitchhikers have been a folklore staple. Many of these stories from our haunted highways even predate automobile travel, which bestows the legends with that irresistible combination of history and mystery. Over the years, the occasional "ghostly hitchhiker" tale has even been written up as a human-interest piece in local newspapers and, less frequently, articles about the intriguing phenomena have appeared in national magazines.

The following tales are examples of some of the phantom hitchhikers who've been seen over the years as they traversed the routes through and around the Rocky Mountains.

The Flathead Lake area in northwestern Montana is home, not only to the legend of the Flathead Lake monster, but also to a mysterious, vanishing hitchhiker. The female apparition is seen on the side of Highway 28 between the towns of Niarada and Elmo. She appears, from a distance, to be thumbing a lift. But when a driver pulls over to offer her a ride, the image vanishes. One man who'd had an encounter with the ghostly hitchhiker related that as he stopped his car for her to get in, he lit a cigarette. By the time he looked up again, the image had vanished without a trace.

No reports exist of that ghost ever actually getting into anyone's car, which makes her quite different from the poignant tale of the male apparition who occasionally appears in the back seats of cars traveling between Conrad and Valier (both north of Great Falls, Montana). He's said to be the ghost of a young man who was killed in a freak accident along that stretch of highway. His spirit, it seems, is still trying to complete the journey that was tragically cut short.

There is an eerie sameness about all the encounters with this particular ghost. He appears out of nowhere and immediately begins to talk to the driver of the car, explaining that he is cold and lonely. Moments later, the image disappears as quickly and mysteriously as it appeared, leaving the poor driver to wonder what he or she had just experienced.

Some time ago, near Helena, the capital of Montana, a local banker was driving alone at night on a treacherous stretch of road through an area known as McDonald Pass. With his peripheral vision he spotted a young girl emerging from a roadside phone booth. Startled by the unexpected sight, the man slowed his car. He soon realized that the girl was waving at him to stop.

Even while traveling through apparently uninhabited areas high in the Rocky Mountains, you may be in for a surprise meeting with a ghost.

He hurriedly pulled off to the shoulder of the road to offer assistance. His car had barely stopped when the girl jumped into the back seat. She was completely distraught, repeating over and over again that her father was worried about her and that she had to get right home. The startled man was glad that he'd stopped. He tried to calm the child by assuring her that he would drive her home immediately if only she would tell him where she lived. She gave him an address on a street whose name he recognized, and he made his way there as quickly as possible.

His good deed accomplished, the banker drove back to where he'd first seen his unexpected passenger and, from there, completed his own drive. The next day he noticed that the child had left her sweater in his car. He promised himself that he'd make a trip to her address as soon as his other duties allowed him time. Several days elapsed before he pulled up in front of the house where he'd dropped the child off. He collected the sweater from where it had been left on the seat, approached the house and knocked on the door.

An elderly man opened the door and listened to the driver's story. Rather than responding with warmth or even, at the least, courtesy, the old man flew into a rage. How could anyone be so cruel, he wanted to know.

When the banker was finally able to get the homeowner calm enough to be coherent, he heard a story that left him permanently chilled. It seems that this old man's daughter had been killed in a traffic accident some years before. It had occurred at the exact location where, just a few days before, the banker had come to the girl's assistance.

Needless to say, both men were badly shaken by the implications of what each one had said—the banker even more so when he learned that the day he'd seen and spoken to the ghost of the distraught youngster was the anniversary of her birthday.

An elderly man is occasionally seen hitchhiking on a section of highway near Jasper in west-central Alberta. Concerned motorists who spot the image pull over to offer the stranger a ride. But, just as they do, the image they so clearly see vaporizes.

Many drivers who experience such an unnerving encounter will come into the office of nearby Sunwapta Falls Bungalows to tell someone what's just happened. By now, staff there have become familiar with the tale. Many of them have even experienced similar sightings. They also know, from what they've seen and from what others have reported, that the disappearing hitchhiker is, in fact, a ghost. More specifically, it is the ghost of the founder of Sunwapta Falls Bungalows, William Hayhurst.

It seems that once people are used to the specter, Hayhurst's spirit is not a frightening sight, for he means no harm to anyone. His continuing interest in the Bungalows is actually most understandable. He began the business during the first years of the Second World War. During this time, the construction process was difficult, as were the first few years of operation. Despite these obstacles and much to Hayhurst's pride, the resort became a success.

At the time of his death, William Hayhurst no longer owned Sunwapta Falls Bungalows. Nevertheless, he has obviously retained an emotional attachment to them for, since his death, Hayhurst's ghost has become an accepted presence in and around the place. His spirit is felt more frequently than it is actually seen but, when his apparition does appear, it's quickly recognized. The staff, of course, have become accustomed to their strange, ethereal visitor. Motorists driving along the highway, however, are still surprised when they see an image of an older man hitchhiking. They're even more surprised when, as befits a legend in this category, the person that they've stopped for vanishes before their eyes.

The Highwood Hitchhiker

In the early 1980s, when Jim and Louise Lutz lived in Calgary, Alberta, they hosted a visit from Jim's sister and her husband. These visitors were from out of the country and they were anxious to see some of the rugged mountain countryside not far from the Lutz home. Toward this end it was determined that the two couples would head out for a daytrip in the Lutzes' four-wheel-drive vehicle. Their destination was McPhail Creek, in the backcountry around Highwood River. They headed south from Calgary to the Longview area and then west to the Kananaskis Road before heading north again. They came to the Cat Creek Campground and then forded the Highwood River. The trail was rugged, but Jim Lutz was a well-experienced driver and the trip was going well.

Just at this point in their travels, they were most surprised to see a young man walking with a black dog. Louise Lutz explained that under such circumstances it never would have crossed their minds not to stop and offer assistance. They opened their car to the fellow who, with his dog, got into the front seat.

After explaining "that his friends got stuck with their vehicle not very far away ... the fellow didn't talk to us or look at us. Neither did the dog," Mrs. Lutz recalled. Jim Lutz advised the stranger, "We're just out on a daytrip, we don't have too much time to spare because we have visitors." The young man assured the good Samaritans, "It's just a short distance."

The Lutzes' guests were feeling uneasy about the young man now accompanying them. Worse, the area that he was leading them to didn't seem to have been traveled over by any sort of a vehicle for a very long time.

Jim Lutz soon realized that this expedition was going to take considerably more time and even more resources than they had available. He informed the young man, "We haven't got time to do this now. I'll take you back across the Highwood River and you can walk to the Cat Creek Campground. When we came by there was a fellow there with a jeep and a winch. He can probably help you."

The Lutzes did exactly that. At the opposite bank of the Highwood River their rider and his dog got out of their car. Moments later, the pair had vanished from sight entirely. Confused, but perhaps also somewhat relieved, Jim Lutz headed back across the river. Unfortunately, his vehicle stalled, midstream, and the Lutzes ended up being the ones to require the help of the man at the campground with the jeep and the winch.

Of course, they inquired as to whether their odd passenger had also been by asking for assistance. "Oh, no," came the reply. "We haven't seen anybody go by here."

For some time after that strange encounter, the Lutzes made a point to listen to stories from people who'd had unusual experiences in that rugged backcountry area. Their attentions were rewarded by tales similar to their own. These stories, however, never included any explanation for either the appearance, or the disappearance, of the mysterious young man with the black dog, except to establish him as an accepted part of the mountain folklore in that area.

Ghost Riders

Harold McDougall and his son, Gary, a photographer from Penticton, British Columbia, were exploring the remote terrain around Elinor Lake in the province's Okanagan area, on an August day in 1984, when they stopped for a trailside lunch. Feeling totally isolated from the world, the pair savored their food while appreciating the complete silence of their surroundings.

To their great surprise, the two men heard the distinctive sounds of horses' hooves approaching along the trail. Moments later, a group of five riders appeared in a nearby clearing. The two oldest, the McDougalls surmised, might have been the parents of the three younger ones.

All the riders were dressed in clothing that was far too heavy for a warm summer's day. The men wore cloth hats, suspenders to hold up their heavyweight trousers, and high riding boots. Their horses' saddles were simple, adorned only by the heavy canvas bags strapped to them. The vision that the McDougalls cast their eyes upon that day was undeniably a strange one. The approaching family's odd appearance was certainly no call for rudeness, so Harold called out a greeting.

This simple gesture appeared to startle the travelers. When the man that the two hikers presumed to be the father of the younger three riders regained his composure, he touched his hat briefly in acknowledgment before quickly leading his little group away from the two men.

More than a little intrigued, Harold and Gary waited just a moment before attempting to follow the family, if only to get a second look that might somehow confirm what they'd just seen.

They hurried to the trail, which was as straight as an arrow at that point. Although they could see clearly for a considerable distance in either direction, they could spot no trace of either the five people or their horses.

Stranger still, as the McDougalls walked along the dirt trail, they noted that their own steps left footprints on the ground, but there was no sign of any prints from horses' hooves. They then realized what, other than being excessive for the weather, was odd about the family's clothing: it was of a style from a much earlier era. For just a moment, apparently, Gary and Harold McDougall were privy to a peek backward, through the curtain of time.

On a farm not far from that location, but many years before the incident described above, two brothers left their house on a snowy winter evening to attend to their chores. When Sam and Edward Richards were finished tending to the horses in the barn, they came outside and noticed a man walking toward them. The lads saw the image clearly and later described it as having been dressed all in white.

Their farmstead home was in the rolling foothills and extremely isolated, so this sight struck both boys as being extremely odd. Thinking that the man had lost his way, they called out to him but got no response. The image merely continued along the path up to the boys' house. The boys followed—or tried to, for seconds later the man that they'd both distinctly seen vanished.

Sam and Edward rushed in to tell their parents of the strange trespasser. Upon hearing their sons' news, Mr. and Mrs. Richards were just as concerned as the youngsters had been. They immediately bundled up and followed the boys out to the yard. There was no one there, nor were there any footprints in the snow.

At their parents' urgings, the Richards boys described the white coat that the image had been wearing. It was finally clear then what had happened. Like the McDougalls in the previous story, the boys had had a firsthand look at the past. They had experienced retrocognition.

The Vanishing Victim

Although not a vanishing hitchhiker legend, this story resembles the earlier ones in this chapter. It also contains enough interesting differences to make it another classic western ghost story. The place was somewhere along the Colorado Central Railroad near Golden, just west of Denver, Colorado. The date was July 21, 1881.

As the heavy steam engine chugged on, pulling its payload of rolling stock behind it, the engineer kept a close watch out the side window of the cab. All was going well until he caught a glimpse of what looked like a bearded man standing on the track just ahead. The engineer fired a warning blast on the whistle and jammed the braking mechanism on as hard and as fast as he could. Despite his quick responses, seconds later he was sickened by the sound and feel of a thud against the engine's front grill. His engine had hit, and no doubt killed, the man on the track.

It took several seconds for the train to slow sufficiently for the engineer to investigate the terrible accident that he knew had occurred. The distraught man probably took those extra moments to compose himself in anticipation of the gruesome sight that would, inevitably, be waiting for him on the tracks. As soon as he safely could, the engineer jumped out of the train and onto the side of the track bed.

At first he saw nothing—no sign that anyone or anything had been hit by the train. But that was impossible. He'd seen the image on the tracks and had felt the jolt as the train had run over it. There had to be a badly pulverized human body somewhere under the train. Perhaps the remains would be back farther than he thought. Still standing beside the track, he signaled his crew remaining in the cab of the engine to back the train up.

As he watched the puffs of smoke from the train recede towards the horizon, he was puzzled. There was nothing on or near the tracks for more than a mile (about two kilometers). He should have found the body but there was no sign that anyone, dead or alive, had ever been on the tracks.

As he stood in a daze of concern and puzzlement, the engineer tried to reconstruct in his mind what had happened. Unfortunately, this mental review served only to add another strange element to the mystery, for he recalled that the image he'd seen on the tracks had been wearing a black coat and hat. It was the middle of summer—such garments would have been, at the very least, unnecessary and uncomfortable. Badly upset by the confusing situation in which he found himself, the engineer signaled his crew to bring the train forward again so that he might resume his post.

The remainder of that trip was blissfully uneventful, as were many that followed it. In a few weeks the engineer was able to begin to put the puzzling incident behind him—just in time for another, equally strange, event.

At the spot where the engineer had been sure that the train had struck and run over the man in black, he heard a disembodied heart-wrenching moan. Seconds later, passengers reported that an image appeared on board—an image of a bearded man wearing a black coat and a black derby hat. The apparition exuded a severe chill and dreadful odor as it made its way through the train car—before disappearing into thin air. Even when the image had vanished, a foul odor clung to the air along the specter's route down the aisle between the passengers' seats.

Some weeks later, Peter Dornin, a Denver businessman taking the train along that Colorado line, reported that a foul-smelling specter had, for a time, sat down beside him. He added that he sensed the presence was not only unnatural, but evil. Dornin's sighting was not the last. With each ensuing visit, the reports of the ghost became more unpleasant. It seemed that the malevolent spirit was gaining strength. Passengers who saw the apparition were terrified. On one occasion, the phantom was said to have been responsible for breaking the lights in a passenger car.

Speculation and concern were rampant among train crews and the general community. The crew members of the train thought to have originally hit the bearded man were especially distraught, for they always felt somehow responsible for the haunting.

The ghostly appearances on the tracks and in the train lessened gradually until the 1920s, when that rail route was abandoned in favor of a modern highway, Highway 93. Over the years, motorists have reported some strange phenomena on Highway 93 near Golden. Apparently an apparition suddenly appears in their car with them—an image of a bearded man wearing a black coat and a derby hat. And then he vanishes—

leaving behind only badly unnerved travelers and a decidedly
unpleasant, lingering odor.

A Vision
of Loveliness

A much more appealing specter frequently rode the trains on
the Atchison, Topeka and Sante Fe Railroad through Colorado
during the late 1880s. This phantom was a female and an
attractive one at that. Her blue eyes sparkled and her raven hair
shone, thereby setting off her shapely body to its best effect. The
phantom smiled prettily, giving every impression that, wherever
she was, she was at peace.

Oddly, railway workers were apparently the only ones who
ever saw this vision of loveliness. No passengers on the line ever
indicated that they'd seen anything out of the ordinary, even
though she frequently appeared in front of them.

She was also seen waiting contentedly on station platforms as
the trains lumbered into town. Sometimes she would disappear
before the cars came to a stop and at other times she would
board. On still other occasions the mysterious beauty simply
appeared in a coach, mid-journey, and stayed for a few moments
and then vaporized into invisibility.

Marshall Pass and the Phantom Train

A frate train was recked as yu saw. Now that yu saw it yu will never make another run. The enjine was not ounder control and four sexshun men wor killed. If yu ever run on this road again yu will be recked.

Engineer Nelson Edwards found that message etched in the frost of his traincab windows the morning after he had an absolutely terrifying paranormal encounter while traversing Marshall Pass in Colorado.

Edwards was no youngster the day that he made his final trip across the expanse of Marshall Pass. He was an experienced train engineer who, even though the bridge over the canyon was new, had uneventfully traversed those rails before. This time, though, he was especially on guard because he'd been warned of problems with the track ahead. Worse, just as the train was approaching its descent, Edwards received a signal to stop. Concerned, he called out to his conductor whom, he presumed, had issued the order. Oddly, the conductor denied having initiated such a request and added that if he were going to suggest a change of speed it would've been an increase. He'd noticed, the conductor hurriedly explained, that there was another train behind them on the tracks. It was gaining speed and quickly reducing the distance between the two trains. The situation was getting more and more dangerous with each passing minute. Speed, the conductor stressed, was of the essence to ensure safety.

Edwards didn't even need to do a quick check in his mirror to verify the information that he was being given. By now he could hear the approaching train's insistent whistles. The dilemma was horrifying. To pass safely over a defect he knew was on the track just ahead, he needed to slow down, but to keep ahead of the pursuing train behind him, he had to push his own train's throttle to the full-open position.

He piloted the train to the summit at as high a speed as he safely could, and then cut off all power. Gravity would do its work from there. As the train barreled down the steep slope, Edwards could still see the light of the train behind him. As it grew closer, it became obvious that the other engine's rolling stock was considerably larger than his own. If the train behind ever caught up, he knew that the drama would end in disaster.

As the trains entered a sharp curve in the tracks, both the conductor and Nelson Edwards could see the engineer of the threatening train—his head was leaning out the window of the

The combination of trains and tragedy in the Rocky Mountains often resulted in ghosts.

cab—and he appeared to be laughing at the badly frightened Edwards.

Onward the two trains sped in their dangerous game of chase. Minutes later, Edwards blinked in disbelief. There, ahead of him on the tracks, was a warning lantern. Now he was being chased from behind and blocked in front. He had nowhere to turn. Slamming the braking lever on full to prevent hitting whatever was on the tracks just ahead, Nelson Edwards prepared for the inevitable collision from behind.

He heard the pursuing train sound a warning whistle and braced himself to meet his Maker. Seconds later, his train screeched to a stop, but the threat from behind didn't materialize. Edwards and his crew watched in disbelief as the train behind approached at a tremendous speed—only to rise above the tracks, then above their own train and on into the air before descending from sight to the canyon below. Edwards, his crew and passengers listened to hear the inevitable screams and crash as the other train hit the bottom of the gulch. But there wasn't a sound. Stranger still, the lantern marking the obstacle that the engineer had stopped for had also disappeared.

The next day, the authorities searched the area for the wreck but nothing was ever found—except that cryptic message on the window of Edwards's engine. Convinced that he'd been pursued by a phantom train—a crisis apparition—the man resigned his post immediately and sought other employment.

The Ghost of Black Horse Lake

A stretch of highway in west-central Montana near Great Falls is home to a modern-day ghost whose history is eerily similar to the story of "The Vanishing Victim" (p. 28). In the 1960s, a woman named Sadie Lippert was driving at night with five friends. In a second car, following right behind, were five other friends of Sadie's, one of whom was a medical doctor.

The drive had been completely uneventful until, out of nowhere, a man's face, filled with a look of horror and pain, appeared on Sadie's windshield. She was sure that the man must have been walking on the road, that she hadn't seen him, and that she had struck him with her car. All of Sadie's passengers saw him as clearly as she did and they too were convinced that the car had hit the man. Oddly, there was no sound associated with the presumed collision.

Sadie brought her car to a stop as quickly as she dared, not wanting to brake too suddenly for fear that the car traveling immediately behind her might run into her. By the time she had stopped, the second car had too. The friend who was a physician had already jumped out of that car and was calling out, identifying himself as a doctor who was able to help the injured. Unbelievably, the driver of the second car had also thought that he'd hit someone—someone fitting the exact description of the person Sadie thought that she'd hit.

No amount of searching turned up any sign of anyone other than the two carloads of badly shaken friends. No damage was evident to either vehicle; there was no sign that anyone had been hit by either car.

Although they didn't realize it at the time, they had just had an encounter with the Ghost of Black Horse Lake.

Sadie Lippert and her friends were certainly not the last to share such a terrifying experience on that piece of roadway. In the early 1970s, a man named Kalanick was driving along Highway 87 on his way from Great Falls to Fort Benton. The trip had been a quiet one until, in the vicinity of Black Horse Lake, Kalanick noticed a man standing in the middle of the road not far from his car. He had only seconds to try to avoid a terrible mishap. Kalanick slammed his foot onto the brake pedal but was only able to stare in horror as his car's momentum hurtled him toward the man on the highway. Kalanick saw the image clearly enough that he was later able to describe the man's appearance in great detail.

The moment the car finally came to a stop, Kalanick jumped out to see how badly injured the man was. No one was there— no sign that anyone had been standing on the road, let alone been hit. The road was clean, his car was undamaged, and there was nothing, except Kalanick's tire marks, to indicate that anything out of the ordinary had just happened.

Kalanick drove on to his destination because staying at the scene of an apparent non-accident seemed purposeless. Days later, though, after pondering his puzzling experience, he began to tentatively mention the occurrence to people whom he dealt with on a daily basis. That was how he learned that his experience had actually been fairly common and that the man whom he'd "hit" was a ghost—not just any ghost, but the Ghost of Black Horse Lake.

The Mysterious Mechanic

For reasons that will become clear at the conclusion of this chilling tale, the names of the people involved in this haunted highway story have been omitted.

The year was 1950. A young couple and their two-year-old daughter loaded what little they owned into an unreliable eleven-year-old car and headed for Sheridan, Wyoming. They hoped to start a new life for themselves there, close to the grandeur of the mountains. Before the trip was over, however, it had become apparent that, had it not been for an incident of paranormal intervention along the way, they might never have made it to their destination—or, for that matter, they might not have even lived to speak of the hardships that they endured during their journey.

It was winter and a blizzard raged. The young husband knew that the drive would be difficult and tension-filled. In preparation for what would no doubt be an endurance test for both his emotional control and his driving skills, he pulled into a service station. He stood shivering beside the gas jockey as the man added antifreeze to the run-down car's radiator. Perhaps just to make conversation or perhaps out of a genuine concern for the little family's well-being, the attendant pointed out a motel not far from where they stood. He added that, in his opinion, this storm was not one to attempt to drive through.

With the cockiness of youth, the husband thanked the man but got back into his car and headed out on the highway to continue the drive. Just minutes later, he noted with relief that both his wife and their baby had fallen asleep. Now at least he'd only have the poor driving conditions to concentrate on. The man settled in for a long and stressful night behind the wheel.

As he drove, the storm worsened. Visibility was reduced to nearly nil. Hoping that some extra illumination would help him to see through the sheets of falling snow, the man switched his headlights to their high beams. The change only made the situation worse, by increasing the amount of light reflected from the falling snow. He quickly went back to the regular headlight setting but, even in just that short period of time, the ferocity of the storm had picked up considerably.

The car's heater had seemingly become less effective. Was it just a result of the rapidly dropping temperatures, he wondered, or was something malfunctioning? There was no time now to dwell on such rhetorical questions. The intensity of the storm had worsened—he was driving almost blind. In a desperate attempt to do something to help himself to get through this ordeal, the now-frightened man decided to change his tactics: if the visibility was *decreased* with the high beams shining, then possibly he'd be able to see at least a *little* farther if he turned off his headlights entirely.

There was an improvement, but not enough to make up for the additional danger that another vehicle on the road would now have absolutely no chance to see his car. In a last-ditch attempt to gain some view of the road ahead, he rolled down his car window and stuck his head out. The wind that had been shaking the car mercilessly now whipped granules of cutting snow at his face. In a perverse way he welcomed the pain— it seemed a suitable punishment for not having had the sense to stop for the night.

Progress was excruciatingly slow, and the man had no idea whether he was in his own lane, in the center of the highway or possibly even in the oncoming lane. Quickly checking his watch, he took some comfort in the fact it was now a little past two in the morning. The time, combined with the road conditions, made it unlikely that there would be any other traffic.

Suddenly the old and overworked engine gave out something that approximated a cough. The car shuddered, wakening the man's wife, and then glided to a halt. The two stared at each other helplessly. Neither knew anything about cars, but they did realize that there was little chance that they would live through the night unless something changed—and quickly.

The man pulled his jacket around him, got out and made his way to the front of the car. He lifted the hood and stared uncomprehendingly into the engine compartment until the severe wind and snow drove him to close the hood and get back inside the vehicle. His wife had pulled more blankets around herself and the baby before drifting back to sleep. What a blessing, he thought as he listened to their sleep-induced deep breaths, if we're all going to die out here tonight, at least let it be painlessly in our sleep.

He closed his eyes, preparing to succumb to the inevitable hypothermia. When he felt—more than heard—the hood of his car being raised, he actually thought that he was hallucinating or, at the very least, dreaming. Stranger still, his eyes, when he opened them, seemed to confirm what his other senses had told him. The hood of his car was definitely up.

Concluding that the wind must have sprung the latch, he groggily got out of the car to close it. There, leaning over into the engine compartment was a shadowy figure. As he moved closer to the image he could hear, through the howling wind, the sound of a screwdriver against metal. The shape that had been hunched over the front of the car straightened up and spoke to the terrified young man. He told the driver to try starting the car once again. Wondering whether he was dealing with a dream or reality, the man did as he'd been told. The engine coughed twice before firing to life.

With tears of relief and joy coursing down his cheeks, the grateful young husband and father got back out of his car to thank the kindly stranger—but the man was gone. There was nothing and no one in front of his now-idling car—no person, no vehicle, not even any tire tracks. The young man stared blankly at a solitary set of footprints in the snow—his own.

Stunned, he got back into the car and drove slowly through the storm until they reached the safety of the first building that they came to—a roadside diner. The man pulled his car into the parking lot. He'd never anticipated appreciating food and shelter quite so deeply.

The relieved young wife and mother thanked her brave husband for having managed to repair the car and get them all to safety. He took the praise without argument, not to maintain her incorrect evaluation of his abilities, but because he knew that the truth would only traumatize her further—by now he knew that they had just been the recipients of supernatural roadside assistance.

Chapter 2

MYSTERIOUS MINES

Sailors, actors and miners may seem to be most dissimilar groups, but all three share a common bond with the paranormal. And that's really not much of a surprise. All three communities attempt to accomplish tasks that verge on the supernatural in scope. Sailors' lives are routinely tossed about by the powerful will of the sea. Actors strive to convince audiences of an unreal reality. Miners, the focus of this next group of ghost stories, submerge themselves in mother earth, hoping to ferret out as much of her vital and valuable core as they are able to and still get away safely. The balance is delicate; and it is easily and frequently knocked askew.

Drama was inevitable from the very beginning. The existence of hidden precious metals is intrinsic to the geological makeup of the Rocky Mountains. Once people arrived, an ultimately dramatic chain of events began. Mining, the act of humans scrabbling away inside the earth itself, was the decidedly strange, but apparently inevitable, end result.

The total absence of light underground is made even more eerie by the beams shining from the lamps on the miners' helmets. They illuminate only a very concentrated area, meanwhile spreading surreal, shadowy, spectral images that dance on the cavern walls.

Any sound made by the miners, or their equipment echoes, producing a veritable chorus of clanking and banging, as though there are dozens more men in the shaft than there actually are. Even when the miners themselves are silent, rumblings from the bowels of the earth reverberate throughout the workings, bouncing unexpectedly from one rough wall to another. Given this distorting atmosphere, it isn't surprising that some phenomenal tales have emerged from the mines in the Rocky Mountains.

Many of the miners who first worked these untapped caches emigrated from mining communities in Europe and the British Isles, bringing their well-established mining folklore with them and, therefore, an expectation that any mine could be endowed with supernatural characteristics. Tiny but vicious supernatural beings called "Tommy Knockers" (or perhaps more correctly, tales of them) arrived in North America with these immigrant miners and, once here, multiplied at an alarming rate. These vindictive little beasts resembled a hybrid of leprechauns and elves, and *were known to hide in mine shafts. The miners believed that these mischievous beings of legend were responsible for the strange sights and sounds underground.*

A particularly nasty mutation among these supernatural little creatures was a "dwarf" reported in a Utah mine. Although he was short, his arms were so long that he could buckle his shoes without bending over. Moreover, he was so strong that he could make his way up a ladder using only his arms. Miners believed that he would kick the rungs out of the emergency ladders placed in the mines as escape routes in case the miners ever had to get to the surface quickly.

Right from the very first mining accident, other paranormal beings— ghosts—began to burrow in the Rockies alongside the miners. Because the creation of each mining ghost implied the loss of at least one miner, it is fortunate that these more "ordinary" ghosts did not multiply at the rate that the Tommy Knockers did. Still, though, it's been said that any mine worth its metals is haunted by the ghosts of dead miners. The following are some of the stories surrounding those ghosts.

Supernatural Silverton

In the days of the Wild West, gold-rush miners used any and every means at their disposal to locate the treasure buried deep within the mountainsides. One of the most inventive and accurate—as was later proven—of these creative methods was a plan implemented by a Scotsman named Edward Ennis. He arrived in Silverton, Colorado, in the summer of 1875 with exact directions to a mother-lode of riches—gold. These directions had been given to him, he explained, by spirits.

Ennis, already independently wealthy, was so sure that his supernatural instructions were correct that he bought out the owners of a particular mining property at more than fair market price. As soon as he owned the land that the spirits had directed him to purchase, he began to dig. Despite the passage of months and then years without success, Ennis never wavered in his determination that he would eventually hit paydirt. He was so convinced that he would come to an enormous cache of gold that he disregarded all the silver veins that he came across in his search.

As the hunt progressed, Ennis continued to receive messages of direction from those on "the other side." They instructed him to dig, for instance, deeper—or lower, or to the right. Once a supernatural communication warned him of an impending flood in his mine and advised him how to prevent lives being lost as a result. As always, Ennis followed the ghostly advice and, just a few days later, a wall crumbled and thousands of gallons of water poured into the shaft. Fortunately, the well-informed mine owner was prepared and was therefore able to get every miner safely to the surface.

Despite his complete lack of success and dwindling personal resources, Edward Ennis continued on his quest until the bank that was financing his enterprise went bankrupt and so, therefore, did he. Ennis died not long afterward, maintaining to his dying breath that he was on the right path and that a huge repository of gold was close to the point where he'd had to cease operations.

Edward Ennis never reached the elusive riches. The determined Scotsman with a bent for listening to phantoms had been all but forgotten by the people of Silverton when, six years later, another emigrant from Scotland arrived in town. Mary Murrel, or "Highland Mary" as she was known, was also, apparently, a person of independent financial means. Like Ennis, she believed that the ultimate gold seam was, so far, just out of reach.

Not content to spend ten years digging like Ennis had, Highland Mary ordered the deceased man's mine shaft to be blasted open. There, just 1200 feet (365 meters) from where Edward Ennis had been forced to shut down his tunneling efforts, was a veritable "Lake of Gold": millions of dollars worth of gold—as well as silver, zinc and copper.

Everyone connected with the mine became wealthy beyond their wildest dreams. The metals were mined down to the last ounce. People finally realized that the spirits that had directed Edward Ennis all those years had been right. According to Mary, those same voices had also guided her undertaking. Stranger still, once the mine's riches had been depleted, Highland Mary Murrel vanished.

Ghosts and mines are closely connected in Silverton, Colorado.

In an intriguing twist on this legend, miners J.C. Dunn and William Quinn discovered a mine near Silverton. They named the mine "the Highland Mary" and credited the find to following the directions given by a ghost.

The New Discovery Phantom

Like the sailors who believe that women aboard ships portend bad luck, most miners are very superstitious about women being near a mine. The ghost of a woman in a mine was, therefore, especially frightening.

For example, the Old Alliance Mine in Utah was haunted by the ghost of a woman on horseback. The apparition was exceedingly beautiful—her manifestations were consistently described as being a "radiant white" color. The ghost, astride her phantom steed, rode through the subterranean tunnels, her long hair flowing behind her. But since such great negative superstitions were associated with women in mines, many a miner sought work above ground after seeing this particular specter. A ghost in a mine was bad enough, but a female one had the power to drive many men into the light.

In the spring of 1879, a female apparition was seen in the New Discovery Mine near Leadville, Colorado. The observation was obviously considered newsworthy, even by the sophisticated folks on the East Coast, for the story ran in a New York City newspaper. Many of those closest to the revelation, the miners themselves, picked up their final pay packets and fled to seek out safer, or at least saner, venues.

Of the miners who stayed behind, a foolish few tried to capture the phantom. They chased after her fluttering robes until her image dissolved and then vanished completely before their eyes. The manifestation seemed to enjoy these pursuits because, the more the miners chased her, the more frequently she appeared. As the men became weary of the game that they were destined to lose, and consequently ignored the ghost, she appeared less and less often, visiting only when the miners had time to pay attention to her.

Over the years, fatal accidents at the New Discovery Mine meant that the ghostly woman was no longer alone in her realm. Without fail, when the "newer" phantoms made themselves known to the living, so did the original specter. The New Discovery Mine was closed years ago and none of the phantoms that haunted its cavernous belly have been seen for a long time. Perhaps they have gone on to their final resting place—or they may be enjoying their eternity in pitch-black isolation.

Moyer Mine Ghost

The Moyer Mine, near the New Discovery Mine in Colorado, was also very haunted. The identities of many of those ghosts were well known to the flesh-and-blood miners who continued to toil away in her inky blackness. Oddly, at least one of the ghosts who eventually populated the Moyer would have remained alive much longer if he'd only heeded the warnings from the ghosts already haunting the tunnels.

A brief examination of the mine's tragic history will explain that sad fact. Probably the first supernatural presences in the mine were the souls of a dozen miners killed in a cave-in. They remained at the site of their deaths, apparently intent on preventing the deaths of others. These ghosts were credited with scaring miners away from areas where disaster was imminent.

Miner Johnny Cumfrey's recorded experience is an example. Young Johnny was finishing his shift at the Moyer Mine and riding back up to the surface. Without warning, the train-like vehicle he was seated in slowed and then stopped. At the same time, Johnny detected the distinct feeling of a presence nearby. He tried to ignore the sensation when, just as it was becoming overpowering, a disembodied face appeared in front of Johnny's. The terrified man jumped from the train and scrambled, under his own power, to daylight. From this safer vantage point, he announced in an extremely loud voice, to assure anyone within earshot, that he would never set foot in the mine again.

Days later, when Johnny's composure had returned, he thought better of his fear-induced employment decision and he returned to his job. Just hours later, he fell headlong down the mine shaft. Incredibly, and beyond all natural laws, he escaped with only a broken leg. It was widely presumed that his life had been spared by the ghosts.

Senator Gallagher, part owner of the Moyer Mine, was not so fortunate. He didn't believe, nor did he like, all this talk about ghosts in one of his financial investments. To prove his point that there was no such thing as a ghost, he went into the labyrinth of tunnels. The spirits within didn't like Gallagher's attitude toward them any more than he liked their existence. The two opposing forces met in the dark tunnel, whereupon a ghost displayed itself for the senator's benefit. Anxious to prove nothing was abnormal about the mine, the politician continued walking—right through the specter and a few steps more—over the edge of a precipice to an instant death.

Gallagher's spirit never left the Moyer Mine and, not surprisingly, he was neither a pleasant nor a helpful spirit. He was even said to murder miners who made themselves vulnerable to his ire.

The presence of this wicked spirit meant that the remaining owners of the Moyer Mine had a very difficult time getting and keeping employees. Those who were brave—or foolish—enough to work in and around those possessed shafts were often very sorry. A night-watchman suffered such terror during his first shift that he enjoyed only infrequent and intermittent moments of sanity afterward. He spoke of having spent the entire shift continuously chasing an elusive phantom light throughout the maze of tunnels. The unfortunate one-time night-watchman died without ever fully recovering his sanity.

Effectively, by scaring away the people able to mine it, the spirits eventually forced the closure of the Moyer Mine.

One-armed Ghosts

In the 1890s, the Cripple Creek area of Colorado was not for the faint of heart. It was coal-mining country, a place where only the strong survived—and some of them were so tenacious that even death wouldn't make them give up.

Many mysterious tales surround the district, but one particular mine, the so-called "Mamie R," has wrought some especially blood-chilling folklore. The mine had earned a gruesome reputation—over the years there had been deaths at the mine and, as a result, many people concluded that the shafts were home to evil, supernatural beings.

In 1894, these rumors were likely not on anyone's mind when the crew at the top of the shaft heard the signal from below to lower the lift device and bring a miner up. The lift operators responded, waited a moment, and then began to raise the bucket. They were most surprised to find it empty. More puzzled than concerned, they put the strange incident out of their minds. A few nights later the signal happened again.

This time, however, the bucket came up with a dreadful load—a fatally injured miner. He looked to be barely alive. One

Coal-mining operations such as this one once dotted the Rocky Mountains. Many miners were sure that there were ghosts and other paranormal presences in and around the eerie, dark shafts and tunnels.

of his arms had been blown off and his face was covered in blood. The workers immediately reached out to help the man, but their hands went right through the gruesome-looking image as though nothing was there.

Seconds later, as they watched in disbelief, the one-armed miner climbed out of the bucket and began to walk away. He only got a few steps before disappearing before their eyes. Stunned silence reigned for a moment, then they agreed to call the miners below to the surface. It was only then that the lift operators learned that the first day that they'd heard the signal to lower the bucket, but no one had ridden up in it, the miners down below had encountered the badly injured phantom for the first time. The image had struggled to the lift, the signal to raise it had been sounded and, as the bucket ascended, the man simply vanished. The miners below had been so afraid that they'd agreed not to tell anyone about what they'd seen.

The awful scene was played out again and again in the coming weeks. Scuttlebutt had it that the mine was not only haunted but jinxed. On Christmas Day in 1894, the miners found the Mamie R's shaft full of water. They used the lift buckets in an attempt to bail it out. As the bucket was being lowered for the thirteenth time, the cable came off its spindle, catching the operator's neck. As his co-workers watched in helpless horror, he was beheaded.

That was enough. The Mamie R at Cripple Creek was closed down for good.

In an interesting addendum to this ghost story, the listings of the Colorado State Bureau of Mines does not show that such a mine ever existed in such a location. A conspiratorial cover-up? Perhaps. If you find that thought uncomfortable, you might be relieved to know that these although these grisly ghost stories date from 1894—and the official records go back only to 1895.

But Cripple Creek and the Mamie R were not the only mining locations in Colorado to be home to a one-armed ghost. Such sightings were also reported at the both the Chippewa Number Six and the Stevens Mines.

The White Lady

This much is known: Latuda, Utah, is a ghost town and has been since its once-profitable coal-mining operation was closed down in 1966. Some folks say that the place is still home to one forlorn soul—"the White Lady." Others are skeptical and insist that the place is *not* haunted at all and that the White Lady is simply a legend dreamed up by area teenagers after the town was abandoned.

Admittedly, some "true ghost stories" have been known to lose their credibility when examined too closely. This one, however, is somewhat different, for it is the skeptics' argument that falls apart under scrutiny. Those who were teenagers in the late 1960s might have been responsible for popularizing the tale, but they certainly didn't create the White Lady, because there are documented accounts of her ethereal existence that considerably predate even the birth of that generation.

Although details of the White Lady's background have become confused over the years, there is agreement that the lost soul was a sorrowful widow. Because of the injustices that she suffered in this life, she's been unable to find peace in the next one. Some folks say that her husband died in a mining accident;

other people have different explanations for her provider's death. Whatever may have happened, it is known that the widow was left destitute and with a child to raise.

The woman's last few years were horrific, although, once again, not everyone agrees as to the details. Some folks say that she died in an institution, having been placed there after killing her child in a terrible attempt to protect the little one from a lifetime of suffering. In death, however, she's returned to haunt the mining town.

Today, only the barest ruins remain of the once-prosperous town of Latuda, but the White Lady doesn't seem to notice the changes. She's apparently frozen in the time when she lived in the town. Explorers, hikers, ghost-busters and others frequently report seeing the image of a woman, dressed in a flowing white gown. She hovers just above the ground before making her way toward what was once the mining office and then disappearing.

A ghost known as "the White Lady" is said, by some, to haunt the ghost town of Latuda, Utah.

In 1972, a young man was so tormented by the sight of the ghost that he blew up a portion of the abandoned and crumbling building. The badly frightened youth paid a high price for his dramatic overreaction to the encounter: a term in jail.

His fate has not discouraged others from visiting the haunted area, for sightings of the ghostly White Lady continue to be reported at the nearby city of Helper, Utah.

The Ghost Wore Yellow

Park City Silver Mine, near Park City in Utah, is said to be home to a ghost clad in a yellow slicker. He roams the dark, dank tunnels of the mine and the building that used to be the Miners' Hospital. Local history has it that the shaft where the man was working caved in, injuring him badly. His workmates were able to haul him to the surface and take him to the hospital. Unfortunately, he didn't survive his injuries but, rather than dying in the bowels of the Rockies, at least the man met his Maker in a sun-filled room on the top floor of a sterile hospital ward.

Shortly after the man's death, other miners reported seeing his image throughout the mine tunnels as they worked. The sight terrified the men. They became convinced that if anyone spoke to the ghostly image, that person would soon die.

The building where the man actually died is now Park City's Community Center. The top floor is set aside as a dormitory for skiers visiting the nearby mountains. Many an athlete has been startled by the apparition in the yellow slicker who is, apparently, roaming the halls into eternity.

Blackjack's Ghostly Legacy

The concept of a "lost mine" has a long, and lethal, tradition in North American mythology. The lore surrounding little-explored territories, such as the Nahanni Mountains in northern Canada, is rich with tales not only of lost mines, but even of wonders such as hidden tropical valleys. In the earliest days of the twentieth century, when such stories made their way to the more populated areas farther south, adventurers began to head north, hoping to find this elusive paradise of geologic wealth and geographic beauty for themselves.

There is no record that these seekers ever found either the fabled lost mines or the unlikely lush valleys, but their treks did enrich the cache of legendary tales. Many of those who set out simply disappeared. Those who did return told wondrous stories of their adventures in the remote and extraordinary North.

Today, a hunt for anything resembling the tropics anywhere near the Nahannis would be recognized as folly, but the existence of valuable mineral finds that have not yet been exploited certainly remains a possibility, not only in the remote Nahanni Mountains, but also closer to home. Perhaps if we only knew where to look, we might find not only these hidden veins of precious minerals but also the ghosts of those who died in their quest for wealth.

One of the most enduring tales from the Rocky Mountains is a legend about a lost mine and those who lost everything in their quest to find it. With great justification, the legend of the Lost Lemon Mine has been called "the great mystery of the Canadian Rockies." As this story has been kept alive now for well over a century, there are, by now, many versions of "the truth." All of them, however, begin in springtime of the year 1870, near Tobacco Plains, Montana, with a party of prospectors setting out on a northerly trek to search for gold.

Upon reaching the Highwood Range, in what would later become west-central Alberta, two men from the group, Frank Lemon and his partner, a man known as "Blackjack," set out on a route of their own. As they made their way along the course of the Highwood River, the pair were gratified to notice *showings*— outcroppings that indicated veins of gold below the surface of the ground that they were traversing.

Not wanting to share their find with anyone else from the original party, Lemon and Blackjack scrambled to gather as many pieces of gold ore as they could. They knew that they would need these samples in order to attract a financial backer, someone to bankroll the operation that they would need to establish in order to take advantage of their fortunate discovery. Once they had collected a sufficient number of ore samples, the pair set up camp for the night. They planned to begin heading back to Montana early the next morning.

Several variations of the tale exist to explain what might have happened next. Some say that Blackjack and Lemon got into an argument that eventually escalated into a physical fight. Others say that the two were on the best of terms when they turned in for the night. What is known for a fact, however, is that by sunrise Blackjack was dead—murdered by his former friend and partner, Frank Lemon. As for Lemon, overnight he had gone stark raving mad.

According to this version of the story, the now badly deranged Lemon left the body of his former friend where it lay and headed, as best he was able, back to Montana. When he eventually arrived at Tobacco Plains, the murderer immediately sought counsel from the local priest and confessed his terrible crime. He admitted that he had murdered his partner out of greed, a desire not to share with him whatever riches were to be found. Lemon no doubt hoped that this confession would free him, not only symbolically from the specter of his deed but, in a very real way, from the specter of Blackjack himself—which, he was sure, had been with him from the moment that he had killed the man.

It would seem that Blackjack's ghost, not wanting Lemon to profit from his foul deed, had decided to spoil his former friend's plan by appearing as a ghost and, literally, frightening Lemon out of his wits. Throughout the long night after he'd committed the felony, Lemon had been terrorized by ghostly moans and the sight of disembodied glowing eyes leering at him. Blackjack's understandably angry spirit tormented the murderer until the guilty man had gone almost completely insane.

After listening to the confession, the priest decided that he had to do something to try to calm the distraught soul of the deceased. Hoping that a proper burial would put the enraged phantom to rest, the priest sent a man named John McDougall north to find and bury Blackjack's corpse. McDougall was successful and, after dropping the remains into the hole that he'd dug, the man decided to pay a small tribute to the deceased by marking his burial site with a mound of stones. Unfortunately, despite all this effort, neither the corpse nor the spirit were laid low for long.

Two young Native braves had followed Lemon and Blackjack from the time that the pair had broken away from the larger prospecting party. They were still in the area and, immediately after the burial, they dug up the corpse and left it for the animals to feast on. Then they rearranged the disturbed earth in a way that they hoped would disguise the fact that a burial had ever happened there. These young braves wanted to erase any evidence that might point other non-Natives to the area of the mine. It wasn't that they wanted the minerals for themselves— quite the contrary. Ironically, the Natives believed that gold was inherently evil and would bring nothing but misfortune. That area, though, was valuable to the Natives for another reason. It was a rich hunting ground and they did not want the newcomers and their mining operation to move in and scare the animals away.

Thinking that he had accomplished the purpose of his trip north, McDougall returned to Tobacco Plains. He was shocked to learn that Lemon was still being tormented by evil spirits and that at times the man actually seemed possessed by a supernatural entity. Gradually, by the following spring, Frank Lemon began to recover from his trauma. Interestingly, he was not made to stand trial for the murder that he had already admitted committing. Instead, he was set up to lead a group of prospectors, including John McDougall, back to the murder site, supposedly the location of rich gold deposits.

The expedition was not successful, for the closer that Lemon got to the place where he'd killed his friend, the more insane he became. Eventually the group gave up and returned to Montana, where they immediately made arrangements to send Lemon to his brother's ranch in Texas. There, it is said, the crazed man lived until his death many years later, never fully recovering from being haunted by the ghost of the man whom he'd killed.

Despite the clear indications of what could happen to a man who tried to get near the elusive treasure, McDougall soon headed back toward the Highwood Range of the Rockies in search of the gold. McDougall never made it back there. He didn't even get close; he drank himself to death at a whiskey-post on the way.

Over the next few years there were other attempts to find the treasure. All ended in disaster—a natural disaster in the form of a terrible forest fire, an additional bout of insanity—and a strange, serious and sudden physical illness. Even the most determined prospectors were beginning to realize that "Lemon's Mine," as the much-fabled riches had become known, was haunted by a spirit that would not allow anyone to get near it.

The next recorded expedition of searchers headed out in 1883. On the second day out, one of the leaders became convinced that evil would befall him if he went any farther and so the attempt was abandoned. Weeks later, one of the two braves who'd witnessed Blackjack's murder back in 1870 agreed to guide a group to the site. The night before they were to leave, the Native man inexplicably died in his sleep. When the dead man's son-in-law tried to bury the deceased, the younger man died too. The ghost's body count continued to mount.

A non-Native named "French" was sure that, at last, he'd located the Lemon Mine and he wrote a letter to a friend explaining that he would be leaving the next day to stake his claim. Immediately after posting the letter, French was the victim of a terrible fire. The building he was resting in burned to the ground, leaving him alive but permanently disabled and incapable of revealing the location of the gold.

Since then, and to this day, hundreds of people have searched for what's become known as "the Lost Lemon Mine." Some, but not all, have died, many under mysterious circumstances, and none has succeeded in finding the riches.

The night before an expedition was to set out in 1912, the adventurers were together in a bunkhouse. Their gathering became louder and louder until, during a slight lull in the racket, the entire group heard a disembodied voice plead with them for some quiet. They wisely took this admonishment as proof that the lost gold's ghostly guardian was still present and therefore abandoned their plans.

Despite years of evidence that clearly indicated that looking for the Lost Lemon Mine was an extremely dangerous undertaking, the search continued. Representatives from both the white and Native communities alike devoted their lives to the fruitless task of seeking the elusive and apparently lethal treasure.

In the 1920s, Bill Livingston (son of Alberta pioneer Sam Livingston—who, by the way, is widely believed to still be haunting his preserved cabin in Calgary) believed that he had an explanation for at least part of the mystery of the Lost Lemon Mine. The younger Livingston was convinced that the gold that Blackjack and Lemon had found was not naturally occurring in that area. He believed that the pair had stumbled upon ore dug from another location and somehow lost by the original prospectors as they made their way home with their find. Although Livingston's theory would account for the fact that, to date, no one's ever found the Lost Lemon Mine, it does nothing to explain the strangely occurring deaths associated with attempts to find it.

Perhaps it would be wise simply to accept that the ghost of Blackjack is still on guard.

Only Images Remain

There is, by now, little doubt that coal mining was responsible for the rock slide that almost wiped out the town of Frank in the Crowsnest Pass area of southern Alberta, in the early morning hours of April 29, 1903. In effect, one entire face of Turtle Mountain crashed down on the sleeping town, killing more than seventy people in its minute-and-a-half-long rage. Seventeen miners dug their way out of the mine, and twenty-three other men, women and children survived the disaster. Few of the bodies were ever recovered and, even today, the lethal rocks remain where they fell, forming a mass headstone.

There is now a government-run interpretive center at the site of the Frank Slide, where visitors can learn the details of the tragedy, observe the eerie geography and geology, and appreciate nature's destructive powers. Employees at the center are forthright about their strange working environment, admitting that the sight is an "unnerving" one.

Both staff and tourists have observed shadowy shapes hovering about the strange, boulder-strewn landscape. People who stop to take photos by the roadside sign explaining the tragedy are often puzzled to find the ghostly outline of an extra image huddled in among the folks whose picture they intended to take.

The debris from the Frank Slide remains as a monument to the lives lost in the tragedy. Presences are often detected among the rubble.

Horrors Sensed

The next Crowsnest Pass town to be hit by disaster was Bellevue, which was near Frank. In 1910, an underground explosion in the Bellevue Mine killed thirty men. The tragedy permanently scarred the psychic landscape of the area, for even today there is an ominous and oppressive feeling near the minesite.

This mass grave holds the remains of the victims killed in the Hillcrest Mine explosion. The area is still oppressed by their spirits.

After Bellevue, the next town in the Crowsnest Pass to be hit by lethal misfortune was Hillcrest. In 1914, 189 miners lost their lives in Canada's worst single coal-mining disaster. Despite this horrible catastrophe, the mining operation at Hillcrest continued to function as a viable commercial enterprise until 1949.

Today, according to Monica Field, a spokesperson for the area, the minesite remains pretty much the way it was left in 1949.

"It hasn't been sanitized at all," Field explained. "I frequently take groups of school children there. Every time I do, I can feel the presence of those miners and their families. I can feel the men's disbelief and the agony of the families waiting at the entrance to the mine."

Few people can visit this area and come away unmoved by the dreadfully haunted ambiance.

The Haunted Winter Quarters

At 10:28 on the morning of May 1, 1900, the Winter Quarters Mine just west of Scofield, Utah, exploded, killing two hundred miners—men and boys. People all around, anyone who was able-bodied enough to assist, did so. They pulled the mutilated bodies of the victims—and, amazingly, a few survivors—from the debris.

Despite the Herculean efforts of the rescuers, it was widely believed that some miners remained unaccounted for. The town's Finnish community, for instance, maintained that fifteen of their compatriots were still missing. Trying to cope with the dead and dying stretched the area's resources to the limit. When suppliers in nearby Salt Lake City were able to send only 125 coffins, an additional 75 had to be shipped from Denver.

Burial clothes had to be ordered and the deceased men were dressed in white shirts, ties and black suits before being laid out in their coffins and delivered to their former homes for mourning. Even the weather seemed attuned to the terrible occasion, as it was rainy and windy and, by the morning of Thursday, May 5, the day of the funeral, the entire area had been blanketed with a spring snowfall. The bodies of the miners were taken to the local cemetery and buried, almost as a group, in the northwest quadrant of the property.

Despite everyone's best efforts, mistakes were, understandably, made. Bodies that had been incorrectly identified went into the ground that way. Grave markers, intended to honor the dead, were made up in such a hurry that most men's names were spelled incorrectly on their monuments.

Other tributes, however, were lavish. Railroad cars filled with flowers arrived from the surrounding areas—as did provisions, money and messages of sympathy.

Unfortunately, the tragedy also served to increase the mistrust between the area's Finns and the rest of the community. The Finns were disparaged because, after the dreadful explosion, they hesitated to return to the mine after it reopened on May 28, 1900. The reason for their hesitancy? The mine was now very haunted, as was the cemetery where so many of the recent victims had been buried.

The following article about the hauntings ran in the *Utah Advocate* on January 17, 1901.

> *The superstitious miners, who are foreigners [the Finns], have come to the conclusion that the property is haunted, inhabited by a ghost. Several of them heard strange and unusual noises, and those favored with a keener vision than their fellow workmen have actually seen a headless man walking about the mine and according to their statements have accosted the ghost and addressed it or he.*
>
> *At other times the headless man would get aboard the coal cars to which mules and horses are worked and ride with the driver to the mouth of the tunnel when he would mysteriously vanish and again reappear in the mine. Many supposedly intelligent men have claimed this and some twenty-five or forty have thrown up their jobs in consequence.*
>
> *These same people and others have seen mysterious lights in the graveyard on the side of the hill where many victims of the explosion of May are buried .... [A]ll efforts to ferret out the cause [of the ghostly sightings] have been fruitless though close observations have been made by reputable citizens of the camp. These lights are always followed by a death so it is alleged by others than the miners who might be disciples of the supernatural.*
>
> *Tombstones where the light appeared have been blanketed but the light remains clear to the vision of those who watch from town. The ghost of the mine is known among the workmen as "Sandy McGovern."*

Perhaps the restless souls are the indignant souls of those who were misidentified.

A Medley of Mining Manifestations

The ghost of a miner killed one morning at the Star Mine near Leadville, Colorado, re-enacted his death by suffocation, and the immediate moments leading up to it, over and over again. The haunting did not stop until the mine shaft was closed. Of course, no proof exists even now that the poor man is free of his grim eternity. We only know that his image is no longer visible, because the area where he died, and where his ghost was seen, has been sealed off.

Two miners who drowned in the Bates Mine at Black Hawk, Colorado, on August 7, 1885, acted as guardians when, some time later, an explosion ripped through that mine. The images of Sebastian Zang and William Vine were observed holding up roof and wall timbers while their flesh-and-blood counterparts escaped to safety.

The ghost of Stephen Pierce, murdered October 23, 1877, at the Mammoth Mine in Colorado, was seen guarding the entry to that mine and has been credited with protecting the lives of the miners toiling away in its subterranean chambers.

Not all violent deaths connected with mines occurred in or around the shafts. Nor were they all a result of accidents. Emotions and economics caused some of the deadly trauma as workers and owners fought about safety and money. To this day in an old mining area near the ghost town of Lincoln, Colorado, the heavy phantom footsteps and raised voices of angry miners are heard plotting to "get the guns from ..." and to "show them who's the boss around here ...." Despite the intensity of the feelings involved, no apparitions have ever been seen, nor have any footprints been left behind.

Not all entities inhabiting mines are ghosts of human beings. A Utah silver mine is haunted by the phantom of a white mule, apparently killed in an underground explosion. The pathetic

An old cabin in the vicinity of Silver Plume, Colorado. Could it have been the home of "Mad Jack"?

animal wanders throughout the abandoned underground tunnels, seemingly unaware that it is no longer living.

Mining has driven more than one man mad. John Strong, or "Mad Jack," as he was commonly known, unintentionally caused his own death in 1859. He'd come to the mountains near Silver Plume, Colorado, with the rush of '49 and shortly thereafter lost his hold on sanity. After Jack had his fatal accident, his friends gave his body a proper burial, but his spirit was not at peace, nor was that of the mule that he was with at the time of his death.

For years afterward, miners swore that they could hear Mad Jack's pickax clinking against the walls of the mine. There were even reports of the ghost of a madman chasing off claim jumpers. Occasionally, too, miners could see a luminous shape near the mine—a shape that resembled a small, horse-like animal.

And so, like actors, whose enchanted world becomes larger than life, and sailors, whose superstitions become reality, miners also lead lives in which supernatural legends are an established component.

Chapter 3

HAUNTED HOUSES

The mechanics of geology that created the Rocky Mountains also, by default, set in motion a series of circumstances that drove some men to premature graves, occasionally in a state of total madness, while allowing others to become wealthy beyond their wildest dreams. The men whom the mountains' inherent precious minerals did bless left a cache of legend-like success stories. The most fortunate of the determined miner-entrepreneurs also left an architectural legacy: mansions—huge, palatial homes, built in the towns and cities nestled in the shadows of the mountain peaks. Many of those grand old houses are now home to ghosts.

Some of the haunted homes in the Rocky Mountains are located on ranches, and many of those ranches, as we shall see in some of the following stories, are haunted as well.

Unsinkable Spirits

A classically American rags-to-riches story began at Hannibal, Missouri, in 1867, with the birth of Margaret Tobin. One of six children, Margaret was raised in abject poverty by uneducated parents. She attended school until she was thirteen. Therefore, when she set out to make her way in the world, she was at something of an educational advantage over her peers, most of whom were lucky if they had stayed in school long enough to learn how to read and write. Perhaps more importantly, Margaret was also ambitious and, by 1886, had made her way from Missouri to the booming mining centers in Colorado.

Here the vivacious young woman met and married thirty-one-year-old James Joseph Brown. "J.J.," as he was most often called, was not only as smart as his bride, but also at least as ambitious. By the mid-1890s, the couple had been blessed with two children and had purchased a family home at a prestigious address.

Both Margaret and J.J. recalled those early days as being the happiest that they'd known. Then their relationship began to splinter, taking much of the enjoyment out of the marriage. Margaret turned her considerable abilities toward social climbing. Her husband, however, abhorred anything even approaching involvement in high society's whirl and the couple drifted apart. They soon made the dissolution of their marriage official.

Margaret Tobin Brown was touring Europe alone in the spring of 1912 when she heard that her young grandson was ill. She immediately made arrangements to return home. The first ship scheduled to sail for the United States left on April 10, 1912. Margaret booked her fateful passage on the RMS *Titanic*.

Stories of her rescue from the sinking ship, as well as her subsequent heroism on that dreadful night, became more and more dramatic with each telling. Hyperbole and Hollywood movies aside, there is no doubt that the woman who had been born to utter poverty and had risen to great financial wealth immediately took charge of the terrified group huddled together in one of the first lifeboats to be launched from the doomed liner. That tragic night, Margaret Brown armed herself with the little craft's oars and rowed the lifeboat and its passengers away from inevitable death.

Her heroics earned Margaret, dubbed "the Unsinkable Mrs. Brown," the publicity that she so craved, but nothing was able to heal the rift in her marriage. J.J., who once told their son, "Your mother is my greatest enemy," died alone in 1922. Margaret also died alone, in 1932.

In death, it would seem that the two have reunited to haunt what was once the Brown family home—their beloved mansion at 1340 Pennsylvania Avenue in Denver, Colorado. The residence is now a museum and is referred to as the Molly Brown House, although during her lifetime Margaret was usually called "Maggie" and never "Molly." The latter name comes from the somewhat fictionalized 1960 stage musical based on her life: *The Unsinkable Molly Brown*.

Despite any variation of her name, there is no question that the unsinkable nature of Maggie Brown's spirit has survived. It is generally accepted by the staff at the museum that the house is haunted not only by Maggie but also by J.J. and the unidentified spirit of a long-deceased servant.

Many people, even casual visitors to the grand old place, acknowledge that they feel the former owners' presence in the rooms. There are also frequent reports of the scent of rosewater, Maggie's favorite fragrance. In addition, there are considerably more direct contacts with the ghost of this most famous of *Titanic* survivors.

Maggie's rocking chair occasionally rocks, independently, for prolonged periods of time. This strange sight is often accompanied by the smell of rosewater.

In the 1970s, when a dance troupe was touring the historic house, a particularly sensitive dancer actually saw Maggie in what had been her bedroom. The apparition was so distinct that the dancer was able to describe the ghost's clothing, right down to the white lace. Maggie's appearance that day was no mere fluke. She had a message that she wanted to get to the curator of her former home. Through the psychically sensitive dancer, Maggie was able to let the staff know to expect delivery of some furniture that had belonged in the home. Less than a month later, someone brought an artifact to the house that had been a part of the original furnishings.

During another tour, a guide was shocked to see a picture on a wall moving. In the October 1996 newsletter from the Molly

"Molly" Brown's unsinkable spirit remains in the home that she loved.

Brown House, the movement was described as "not up and down, not side to side, but sort of rippling forward and back." The guide who reported this strange motion had just launched into an anecdote explaining Maggie's parents' extreme poverty during her childhood and how it resulted in her determination to provide a comfortable lifestyle for her family. The picture that responded to her statements was of the shack where Maggie had been raised. It's likely that the phantom drawing attention to the picture was that of Maggie herself, although it could also have been the ghost of her husband, J.J., whose presence is frequently detected by the smell of cigar smoke wafting through the house.

One of the most puzzling ghostly pranks at Molly Brown House occurred during the Christmas season in the mid-1990s. Decorations in the house included a set of toy soldiers placed under the Christmas tree. The day after they were set out, a volunteer opening the house in the morning found the soldiers lined up, one to a step, ascending the staircase. Thinking that a child visiting the house might have been responsible for the rearrangement, the volunteer worker collected the little soldiers and put them back where they belonged (or so she thought)—under the tree.

As the day progressed and other staff members arrived at the house, the woman made a point to ask each one if he or she had placed the toys on the stairs. No one she asked seemed to know what she was talking about. Only mildly frustrated by the strange occurrence, the woman went about her day.

If she'd forgotten about the incident by the end of that day, what she found the next morning certainly brought all her confusion right back, for there, as though marching up the stairs, were the toy soldiers that she knew had been under the Christmas tree when she had secured the house the night before. This unexplained activity continued for several days. Whoever or whatever was at work through the night in the Molly Brown

House evidently wanted the toy soldiers on the staircase. No one was ever able to solve the puzzle of the toys' mysterious movements during that holiday season.

The ghost with the bent for redecoration might not have been Maggie or J.J.—even in their lifetimes, the Browns already knew that the house had at least one haunted staircase. Maggie's mother once reported seeing the image of a deceased servant on the back staircase. That spirit is apparently still in residence for, in recent years, someone carrying supplies down that stairway was pinched by invisible fingers. There may be some question as to the identity of that ghost, but there is certainly no question that the Molly Brown House is haunted.

Haunted Apartment to Let

This next ghost story took place in the west-central Alberta town of Banff during the 1990s. Donna and John, who have asked that their last name not be used, live in Edmonton with their four children. Donna runs a business and John is engaged in a successful professional practice. They are active, intelligent people, well aware of life's realities and not given to flights of fancy.

My family has known John on a casual, but ongoing, basis for more than twenty years. One day he surprised me with the comment, "My wife wants you to call her." He quickly added the rider, "She has a ghost story for you." I did call Donna and she certainly did have a ghost story for me—one of the most dramatic that I've ever heard.

In 1991, when Donna decided to expand her Edmonton business, she chose a location in the mountain resort town of Banff. Because operating this store would mean that she'd have to spend time away from home, Donna rented a large two-story apartment in Banff. To give me an idea of the size of the suite, Donna explained, "It was the top of a whole building—the place slept twelve."

Donna's background is in health care and so it's not surprising that the first part of settling into her home-away-from-home involved cleaning the apartment thoroughly. With that chore accomplished, she began to stay in the Banff apartment one day a week. Because the place was so big, and her stays there so limited, Donna rented one of the downstairs bedrooms to a business associate while she retained a large upstairs bedroom. The first few months passed uneventfully. Then, without warning, the first in a long list of strange and frightening events occurred.

"I began to hear noises coming from the roof," she explained. "It sounded like a team of guys stomping and dragging chains across the gravel roof."

Although the noise disturbed her, Donna ignored it as best she could until one afternoon when her husband, John, accompanied her on the trip from Edmonton. They arrived tired from their long drive and lay down to have a nap. Before Donna could drift off to sleep, the noises on the roof began once again. Wanting to explain that this cacophony was a regular disruption during her stays in Banff, Donna turned to John. More than a little surprised, Donna stared at her husband lying beside her—he was fast asleep, apparently oblivious to the racket going on overhead. As the next few months were to disclose, this incident was the first in a series for which other people were present but that usually only Donna seemed to be attuned to.

Even with one full-time tenant and Donna's weekly visits, the apartment in Banff was still very much under-used. So, when Mary, her store manager, needed a place to live, Donna arranged for the woman to take one of the empty bedrooms. This bedroom was, like Donna's, also on the second floor and also right below the roof, but Mary never complained of the noises that disturbed Donna. Strange as it seemed, Donna was apparently the only person hearing the racket, and even the timing of her experiences was limited. "I only heard the chains on the roof if I tried to sleep," she acknowledged, before adding, "Then came the smell."

Foul, intense odors that pervade an area for varying durations of time are frequently associated with a haunted place. Knowing that the place was scrupulously clean, Donna was puzzled and annoyed with the malodorous addition to her apartment. Worse, as with the noises from the roof, Donna seemed to be the only one aware of the smell.

"I used potpourri to combat it, but that didn't solve the problem," she recalled. The foul smell was so strong and had such a sudden onset that it seemed to her that, "instantly you were in the middle of it."

Finally, the store manager also became aware of the terrible odor, which Donna described as smelling like a combination of rotten meat and feces. The smell seemed to be concentrated in another big bedroom, and the two women wondered if possibly the vents in the room were bringing in the hideous odor from another part of the building. They checked out this possibility and found that their theory was incorrect.

So far, whoever or whatever Donna was unwittingly sharing her apartment with had tried sound and smell to get her attention. The next sense that the spirit appealed to was sight. Donna set up the scenario for me by describing the design of the kitchen. Exterior light to that room was provided by a skylight in the ceiling, and the kitchen doors were accented with gold-colored glass.

"I arrived one night about eight," she recalled. "It was a very black night. [As seen from outside,] the windows were all aglow with gold, as if my bedroom lights were on and shining through the gold glass."

This sight surprised and concerned Donna, because she presumed that the apartment would be empty when she arrived. Understandably nervous, the woman entered the building making as much noise as possible, hoping that her entrance would scare off the intruder that she feared was inside. The place was empty. Empty of people, that is, but filled with the foul odor. By the time that she reached the kitchen, the golden glowing light that she had seen from the outside had disappeared.

On another occasion, Donna and John invited a group of their friends for a ski weekend. Donna was the first one awake in the morning. She tidied the place up a bit and plugged in the coffee urns. As she walked through the apartment, she was mortified to realize that the now-familiar stench saturated the air yet again. She knew that the place was clean. She also knew that her friends would be astonished by such an odor in one of John and Donna's homes. After all, these people knew Donna and John well. They knew Donna's obsession with cleanliness—some had even dubbed her "Mrs. Clean." But here she was, offering hospitality to friends when there was obviously filth somewhere in the place. Nothing but filth could account for a smell this rancid. Oddly, this time it was concentrated under the staircase.

When the guests rose a little while later, however, no one commented on anything out of the ordinary. They seemed completely unaware of any sort of a smell. As puzzled as she was relieved, Donna set about enjoying her weekend of camaraderie and skiing.

Several months later, Donna was asleep in her home in Edmonton. She began to dream of the place in Banff and the horrid smell that she so often had to endure when she stayed there. In her dream, she was determined to track down the cause of the stench.

"I opened my tenant's bedroom door. A sheet of strong odor hit me," she described. "It was so strong my eyes were watering. Then, for the first time, I'm thinking 'It's a body.'"

In her nightmare, Donna made her way through the man's room. "The end of the bedroom leads to an open area. The smell was even stronger there," she recalled.

Continuing the saga of her nightmare, Donna told me that she swung open the door to the attached bathroom and watched as a horrific scene unraveled before her. "The door hit a bloated body. I saw it through the mirror above the vanity. The body burst and splattered all over the wall. I backed out of the room and telephoned the guy who rented the room. I asked him, 'Did you give anyone the key?' He said he hadn't. I hung up and called the police."

In Donna's dream, the police arrived to find her standing, frozen and mute, pointing to the bedroom door.

At last, Donna was released from her terror by the return of consciousness. "I woke up panting from the terror," she recalled. "I looked at the clock radio and it was 2:49 [AM]."

Now, whatever inhabited Donna's Banff home had made itself felt to her even when she was not staying there. What she didn't know at the time was that a frightening experience had also just occurred to Mary, the store manager who was living in the Banff apartment. Mary had been fast asleep when she had felt a hand on her face. She awoke in terror to find herself alone in her darkened bedroom. The only light came from the luminous dial of the clock radio. It read 2:49 AM.

Perhaps the worst aspect of the two terrifying experiences was that, despite their friendship, both women were so shaken by their experiences that they could not bring themselves to discuss the strange events for a long time. It was many months later that they finally were able to confide in one another and at least find some sort of solace in knowing that they had both had related experiences.

Mary had circumvented the possibility of ever being exposed to that dark terror again by never staying another night in Donna's haunted apartment. For Donna, moving was not an option and so her experiences continued.

On another trip to the mountain town, Donna was alone in the apartment. She was in bed in her large room. In addition to the queen-sized bed where Donna lay, there were a set of bunkbeds and a single bed (which was used by her daughter when she stayed in Banff) in the room. As she lay in the dark trying to drop off to sleep, Donna felt a presence in the room. She turned on the light. There was nothing there, at least nothing that she could see. Donna moved to the middle of her bed. Neither the light nor the move helped.

"I had a feeling of impending doom. I moved to my daughter's single bed. I shoved it up against the wall," said Donna, remembering her attempts to protect herself from an unseen evil. Eventually the feeling lessened and finally disappeared. During that experience, no rancid stench was evident.

Even with her long-suffering nature, Donna had coped with nearly enough by now. Unfortunately though, the entity wasn't through. Donna went on to explain, "It shoved me on the shoulder. I was in the dressing area [of the main bedroom], walking toward the bathroom and someone shoved me. It was a sharp push."

The feeling of being shoved is an unpleasant experience at any time, but decidedly worse when you know for a fact, as Donna did, that you are the only person in the room.

Living, even part-time, in a place that is haunted by something so clearly evil had taken its toll. Donna asked some locals about the history of the building that housed the strange suite.

"It was a bad story. There'd been a little house on the land before. An old alcoholic lived there with his son. The [older] man died in the house. I think it burned down," she recalled.

That information triggered Donna's memory of her horrible nightmare about finding the body. "I think the body [in the dream] had its hands tied behind its back. Someone's got to investigate," she concluded.

Would Donna herself take on the research? "No. I became so afraid that I got rid of the [apartment]."

And so, somewhere in the town of Banff, is there still an unavenged murder victim trying to draw attention to his unnatural end, or has the force exhausted itself by now and the man's spirit gone on to its eternal rest? Perhaps someone reading this account will be able to answer that question.

The Mistress of the Manor

A seventeen-room mansion in Taos, north-central New Mexico, comes equipped with something of a supernatural security system—ghosts, lots of ghosts. The most recent ghostly guard is the spirit of Mabel Dodge Lujan, a long-time owner of the 130-year-old house. She died in 1963 and her presence has never left the place—even after it was requested to do so by a visiting psychic.

In life, Mabel demonstrated herself to be an hospitable hostess by opening her home to artists and writers. In death, she's occasionally shown less endearing qualities. Despite this difference, there's no question that it is Mrs. Lujan's ghost who has been responsible for at least some of the hijinks around the old house, for her image has been seen as a shimmering array of white light. She's credited with pulling the sheets off some sleeping guests and making enough noise to waken others.

Once Mabel frightened playwright Roberta Meyers by emphatically informing Meyers that the play that she was currently working on—which was about Mabel Dodge Lujan's life—did not belong to Roberta, as the writer, but to Mabel herself. Later, Roberta's husband had a dream in which Mabel held tightly onto his wrist. Perhaps it was intended by the phantom to emphasize her spectral point, because when the man awakened in the morning, he was bruised in that area.

Mabel is not alone in her former home's ghostly realm. Even when she resided there as a living being, she was aware that the place was haunted. In the mansion's Rainbow Room, people have often seen the image of a youngster who died of natural causes within it. She's never bothered anyone, beyond giving them a start as they realize that the misty presence that they're seeing in the corner is a manifestation of someone long dead.

In another room there is a considerably more disturbing apparition—a disembodied head. This unnerving sight has been repeatedly documented over the years. Surely one glimpse of such an image would cause a burglar to rethink his or her career choices.

Noisy, Smelly Spirits

Santa Fe, New Mexico, also has its share of mansions and some of them, such as the grand place described below, are haunted.

This particular haunted house dates back to the early twentieth century. In the years since then, the place has in turn served as an enormous private home, offices, a collection of small apartment suites and now, an inn. No one knows how it became haunted, but it is believed that the ghosts who once tormented the people living and working in the place are now gone.

Records of the haunting date back to the 1970s, when a couple and their small child lived in the house. They might have been living there still if the ghostly activity had not forced them to move out. And getting that move accomplished was no easy feat. The husband and wife began their preparations to move out in an orderly fashion, packing their possessions into boxes, one room at a time. Unfortunately, the very ghosts that were driving them away from the house did not seem to want them to move: when they returned to a room that they had left full of packed cartons, they would find the contents completely emptied out.

Despite the make-work project that the ghosts were creating, the couple and their child finally succeeded in getting organized and moved out. The disruptive spirits, however, stayed on to disturb the next tenant, a man named Andy, who moved into the place in 1980, never suspecting that he would be sharing the premises with some very active and annoying ghosts.

The specters didn't wait long after Andy moved in to make themselves known to him. Phantom noises began the very first evening that he spent in the house. Because it sounded like someone was in the apartment below his, and because he knew that that space should've been empty, Andy called the police and reported a burglary in progress.

Before the help that Andy so badly wanted could arrive, the noises began coming from the area above him as well. Shortly afterward, the racket became almost deafening and the young man phoned again for help, but this time he was not able to hear the person on the other end of the phone over the sounds. Seconds later, a dreadful, sickening smell invaded the room. Fortunately, the police car arrived at almost the same time and Andy, badly distraught, began to make his way down the stairs to greet the officers.

As he stepped outside his own apartment, he distinctly heard the door of the suite below his open and then, quickly, close again. Badly frightened, but determined to get downstairs, Andy tried to console himself with the fact that he could see that there was no one else in the stairway. Despite this knowledge, he clearly heard footsteps ascending toward him and, seconds later, felt a draft as though someone had just walked past him on the stairs. Accompanying this decidedly unnerving sensation was the awful smell again, stronger this time. It was a smell that Andy later described as being similar to "rotted meat."

The police searched the entire building, but found nothing. This lack of a visible presence apparently did little to console Andy. He spent that night, which would have been his first in his new apartment, not there but at his parents' home. He only felt safe to return to his suite the next day and, when he did, he was shocked by the sight that awaited him. Every large potted plant in the place, and there were many, had wilted. A closer examination revealed that they had all been frozen.

The second night the sounds were even louder. Andy repeated his phone calls for help—first to his parents and then, after they'd driven him to the safety of their home, to the police. The officers who responded to the call later reported that lights on both the second and third floors of the empty house were blinking on and off. Stranger still, these lights seemed to be moving in a pattern, from room to room and floor to floor.

Each night for the first week of his lease, Andy tried to stay overnight in his flat. Each night he ended up fleeing to his parents' house. The stress was taking its toll on the young man. He did not want this phantom to get the best of him and yet, clearly, it was.

Wondering if perhaps the angry presence was taking advantage of him because he was alone, Andy arranged for two friends to move in as roommates. This change did alter some aspects of the haunting, but not for the better. Now, three people saw, heard and smelled the increasingly gruesome paranormal activity.

The electric lights throughout the building acted independently of human control. Toilets flushed when no one was near them. Andy and his friends watched in silent horror as doorknobs turned and doors opened, to reveal—nothing. The sickening odors became both more terrible and more pervasive. After just a few days, the unexplainable activities drove Andy's roommates to seek other accommodation.

Not wanting to stay alone, Andy sought the company of another friend, a man named Ken. When Ken moved in, he brought his pet cat. However, the poor cat had an even more extreme reaction to the apartment than any of the humans did. It would stand in an apparently empty room, staring intently at something before arching its back, puffing out its fur and hissing at whatever only it saw.

I have heard it said that ghosts like empty buildings because people (live ones) bother them—more, in fact, than ghosts bother people. In the case of this haunted house I wonder if that was the case, for, by now, the spirit was clearly angry. It evidently wanted Andy and everyone else, out of "its" domain and its campaign continued.

If either Andy or Ken put a record on the stereo, an invisible hand would lift the needle arm up and then turn the machine off. On one occasion, phantom gusts of wind began to blow through the apartment, sending papers and other small objects flying about. After that particular incident, the windows were all checked and found to be tightly closed. Next came disembodied and distant voices, followed by the sounds of mirthless laughter and horrible crying. Finally, an apparition, in the form of a filmy female figure, appeared.

A clairvoyant who visited Andy asked if she could look through the place. Her report confirmed what anyone who'd ever spent any time in the house already knew: it was indeed badly haunted. The medium saw three spirits—two women and a man. The older of the two women felt trapped in the house and was very angry at not being able to break free. The other two entities were merely stranded, reliving their before-death lives.

The clairvoyant's report deeply distressed Andy. He had taken just about as much as he could. When he found a priest who was interested in the situation, he was most grateful for the man's offer of assistance.

As Andy and a friend watched, the priest with whom he'd spoken, accompanied by two other clerics, walked slowly through the entire building. They sprinkled holy water and chanted blessings as they went. That night was the first peaceful one that Andy had spent in the old Santa Fe residence.

Despite the newly acquired calm, Andy was more than ready to move on. He found a new apartment and began to pack his belongings in anticipation of moving. The chore was not to be a simple one, however, for, like the tenants before him, Andy's moving cartons were unpacked by unseen hands immediately after he'd packed them.

In an odd coincidence, the haunting presences may well have finally moved out when Andy did. Shortly after he moved on, the place was purchased by a couple. They have turned the nearly century-old, formerly haunted house into a successful (and apparently unhaunted) bed-and-breakfast establishment.

The Ferris Mansion

Every community has one—a house that's reputed to be haunted. There needn't necessarily ever have been any actual encounters with ghosts in the house, it just looks like it *should* be haunted. The myths that develop around such places are generally great fun, especially if the house is abandoned. Sneaking into a supposedly haunted house often becomes a rite of passage for the community's youth, and people of all ages have fun spinning scary yarns for one another using the well-known piece of real estate as the venue for the fictional ghostly activity.

Every now and again, however, such a supposedly haunted house really is home to ghosts. The Ferris Mansion in Rawlins, Wyoming, is such a house. The enormous three-story Victorian-era house has a rich history of ghosts.

The residence was completed in 1903, at great expense—not just financial but, tragically, in lives: several workers died on the job during its construction. Worse, when the work was finished and the Rawlins family moved in, the tragedies continued when little Cecil Rawlins was accidentally shot to death by his brother. Newspaper records of the time confirm that the boy died in 1904, at the tender age of nine. This sorrowful background effectively set the stage for the hauntings that were to come.

The years went by and the Ferrises, who were once among the richest families in Rawlins, moved on. The mansion was sold and soon afterward it was subdivided into apartment suites. Over the years, many tenants reported supernatural goings-on such as a balloon moving across a room as though being pulled on an invisible string by an equally invisible hand. Another tenant related that her tube of toothpaste suddenly flew off the counter, although no one was near it. A young man witnessed sourceless shadows walking past doorways.

The ghostly pranks were never malevolent, but they were mischievous, much like the capers that might be expected from a nine-year-old boy. A painter who lived in the old mansion for a time had a frustrating time keeping track of her painting supplies. Defying all logic, they would go missing—only to turn up later, right where they should have been all along.

Years later, the building was sold again, but this time to be refurbished to its original grandeur. This restoration seems to have pleased the spirits, for they've been quiet ever since.

The Hennessy House

In Butte, Montana, the spirit of D.J. Hennessy, Esq., is thought to linger in the mansion that he built. Although Hennessy's millions were not made directly through mining, his retail chain would not have been the financial success that it was without the miners and their money.

The Hennessy Mansion is once again a single-family residence, but the building has served many purposes through the years and not all of its occupants have treated the home with respect. When a couple named Georges bought the place, it was dreadfully run down and in need of restoration.

After they began the necessary restoration work, they noted that in certain locations around the house there was the distinct feel of a presence, even when they knew that they were alone. At first those feelings were restricted to small areas within the house but, as the work progressed, the number of places where the couple detected invisible company increased. By the time that they began to bring suitable pieces of furniture into the house, the spirit was so pervasive that a man staying in the house actually had to speak out loud and ask the entity to please leave him alone, that he was becoming unnerved and unable to accomplish the household chores that he needed to do. Perhaps not wanting to interfere in any way with the efforts that were finally being devoted to his home, the ghost of D.J. Hennessy immediately obliged.

When Hennessy's presence is not detectable in the old mansion, it may be visiting elsewhere, perhaps with the female apparition who also inhabits the house. She's been seen only in a particular second-floor bedroom. Although her presence has been reported many times over the years, she has never attempted any more-personal contact. She apparently prefers to simply appear in the room, often sitting on the bed, before vanishing as quickly as she came.

The Senator's Spirit

A home known sometimes as "the Copper King Mansion" and at other times as "the Clark Mansion" shares some characteristics with the haunted house in the last story. This enormous residence is also in Butte, Montana, and is firmly believed to be haunted by the original owner.

W.A. Clark was influential politically as well as financially. At the time of his death, he was Senator Clark. Unlike Hennessy, Clark made his wealth directly from mining. Clark's continuing presence in his former home is one of the most treasured aspects of the building, according to its current occupants.

Clark's ghost has occasionally even been seen. Those witnessing the manifestation describe it in almost classic ghost-sighting terms—a flash of either shadow or white moving in a floating fashion.

Everyone associated with the huge home indicates that Clark's spirit is a positive one, but the presence can be something of a nuisance. What is now the game room, for instance, will not warm up past 68°F (20°C), although the rest of the place is a toasty and consistent 78°F (26°C).

Interestingly, Clark's ghost is respectful of the dignity of those still living, in that he will not allow a bathroom door to remain open. Even when the door is purposely propped open, just a little while later it will be found closed. And the phantom's tinkering with doors doesn't end there—he's been known to close doors to other rooms too, and even to lock them.

In common with many other haunted houses, the electric lights at the Clark Mansion can be a problem. Lights that were carefully turned off at night will be found burning brightly the next day.

If all of this ghostly activity were not enough for the Clark Mansion, in a photograph taken in 1990, a phantom image of a sailing ship appeared reflected in a top floor window. However, nothing but blank window glass was visible when the photographer took the picture. Perhaps the Senator's spirit is not the only mysterious force at work in the Clark Mansion.

The Ghost Ranch

There's no question that the Ghost Ranch near Sinker Creek in southwestern Idaho is haunted. The debatable points are simply who haunts the place and how long it has been haunted. Some say that the ranch is possessed by the evil spirits of either Dick or Sally Thomas, and those folks just might be correct. There's also a possibility that the mysterious disappearances of Mr. and Mrs. Thomas themselves might actually be attributable to a different spirit with an evil agenda—one that has resided in the area for a very long time.

The facts of the story follow. As the principals are no longer around to answer questions, we must, from the remaining specifics, each draw our own conclusions.

In 1881, Dick Thomas was twenty-five years old. He'd immigrated from England to profit from the mining opportunities in the Rocky Mountains. Sally, presumably, was close to her husband's age. That she was a friendly young woman is known for sure. Some folks might have gone so far as to say that she was too friendly. Those holding with that opinion were decidedly surprised when Thomas decided to marry her.

Despite the gossip, the two settled down to ranch life in the foothills. The isolation of their homestead didn't prevent word of their frequent and violent quarrels from getting out. Many people in nearby Silver City were well aware that the Thomases had a rocky, and noisy, relationship. The pair split up and then got back together again more times than anyone cared to count. On more than one occasion, Dick accused Sally of attempting to murder him. Theirs was clearly not a match made in heaven.

The marriage continued along this bumpy road for fifteen years—until the spring of 1896—when neighbors noted that both Sally and Dick had not been seen for a while. Upon investigation, it appeared that the two had, to all intents and purposes, disappeared off the face of the earth. At the deserted homestead, however, everything seemed to be pretty much in order. The couple's horses were all in the barn, as were the saddles and wagons.

The interior of the house gave every indication that the people who lived there did not intend to be away for any length of time but would be back at any moment. The table was set for a meal and food, now spoiling, filled the pots on the stove. Dick's wallet lay on a chair and the couple's clothes were in the closets—all except Dick's good suit which, oddly, was missing.

Thoroughly confused, the members of the search party broadened the scope of their efforts to the surrounding land. On the nearby riverbank, they found the body of the couple's dog. Someone, or something, had crushed the poor animal's skull. By now, everyone knew that the sheriff, a man named John Joyce, would have to be called in, and he was. Joyce determined that Sally had tried to buy a large amount of poison not long before the couple disappeared. Many folks immediately jumped to the conclusion that Sally had murdered her husband before sneaking away to a fresh start in life.

Two subsequent developments knocked substantial holes in that theory. The first was when well-respected men from the area began believing that they were seeing Dick Thomas in various parts of the Northwest. Although these sightings were some distance from Sinker Creek, the people who claimed to have seen Dick reported that they were sure of the person whom they'd seen and that he most assuredly wasn't dead.

The second determinant in Sally's innocence was unearthed in 1898—a skull found on what had been the couple's property.

Physicians readily identified it as belonging to a middle-aged woman who had been dead at least two years. With that declaration, Sally Thomas's name was effectively, albeit posthumously, cleared.

Sally's sister and her husband, the Murphys, took over the Thomas ranch not long after it had been vacated. Although they probably weren't immediately recognized as such, signs of a haunting began almost as soon as they moved in. And those signs were not benign. An angry presence was definitely at work.

One day, Mrs. Murphy was knocked unconscious when a rock hurled at her struck her head. Mr. Murphy searched the surrounding area but was not able to find any indication that anyone had been on the land.

When, the following autumn, the couple's hired man went missing, the Murphys decided that they'd had more than enough of living on that ranch. They moved to the city. The move didn't prevent them from hearing about the partial corpse found near their former home. Neither the disappearance of the hired man, nor his apparent murder, were ever explained but, by then, locals had dubbed the place "the Ghost Ranch."

This designation, of course, caused the value of the property to plummet which, in turn, made it an attractive investment opportunity. A family named Brooks bought the place for a song and settled in, just as the Thomases and the Murphys had done before them. The Brookses stayed only until the day after their son had gone to investigate strange noises coming from the barn. The young man never returned from his mission. His parents found him dead on the barn floor. His skull had been crushed. Owning the property no longer held any appeal for the Brookses. They sold the place and immediately put as much distance as possible between themselves and the Ghost Ranch.

Strange stories about the ranch, verging on the supernatural, continued to circulate well into the early twentieth century, but not all of them had tragic overtones. A man named Jack Hunt reported that, when he arrived with his horse-drawn wagon at a barn near the haunted ranch, an invisible stable-hand helped him to unbridle his horses. This unsolicited and unseen assistance frightened him so much that he ran to the nearest occupied house. Jack, and the men who accompanied him back to the barn, were aghast to see that, in the few minutes that it had taken Jack to round up the others, all the remaining horses on his team had been tended to and put away for the night in their stalls. No explanation for the mysterious good deed was ever found.

In another account that involves a ghostly good deed, two men, Williams and Bergh, camped near Sinker Creek one night and built a small sagebrush fire for warmth. Since they expected it to last only a few hours, they were puzzled that it kept burning well into the following morning, because neither man had been awake during the night to add wood.

So, whatever or whoever possessed this foothills ranch back in the late 1800s may have been predominantly evil but was apparently capable of at least some kindness—or there could have been both evil and kindly spirits at large in the area. In any event, this haunting is so well entrenched in area folklore that it is spoken of to this day. There are many who firmly believe that the ghosts of Dick and Sally Thomas still haunt the area. An investigation of the history of the land before the Thomases came to own it, however, confuses the situation considerably.

In an article in *True West* magazine's October 1998 issue, writer Hank Corless makes the following statement about the location of the ill-fated ranch. It was, he writes, "the site of several early-day tragedies, including the destruction of an entire wagon train ... in 1860."

Such a piece of information should perk up the ears of any true ghost hunter. Is the Sinker Creek site haunted by either

Sally or Dick Thomas—or were they also victims of a terrible presence left behind by some earlier fatal disaster? After all, their dog had met a fate similar to what befell the Brooks boy and their own disappearances were, in fact, only two in what became a series of mysterious departures.

As with most ghost stories, many questions remain unanswered. The fact remains that a very unnatural presence haunts the well-named Ghost Ranch.

Accommodation to Let, Furnished and Haunted

In the Rocky Mountains of southeastern British Columbia there is a ghost in residence at a house near a school in an isolated community. Because of its proximity to the school, it has often served as a teacherage—for those educators willing to share their accommodation with a ghost.

No one might ever have heard of this particular haunted house had it not, during the summer of 1957, been occupied by a world-renowned artist. The man, who has asked for anonymity, put up with all the ghostly activity in the tiny place because its beautiful mountain surroundings meant that he had more subjects than he could possibly paint, and because the lakes nearby were well stocked with the fish that he loved to catch.

The artist and his wife leased the house furnished. All they had to do was move in. Even at first, they found one piece of furniture a bit unorthodox—the exterior shell of a grandfather clock, without the clock mechanism. Despite there being no workings inside this clock, it would chime every evening at a particular time. Just when the couple became used to this impossibility, the sounds began to be accompanied by doors throughout the house slamming closed—but there were never any drafts or people about to cause such a thing.

Although all of this unexplained activity in one little house must have had an unsettling effect on the artist and his wife, they stayed on until September, when their tenure was up and two teachers were scheduled to move in. The new tenants decided to rearrange the furniture in the little place. Their decorating ideas must have struck a responsive chord with the resident spirit, for he began to play the piano in the middle of the night. That was enough for the teachers. They fled the haunted little house and refused to ever return.

Oldtimers in the nearby town suspected that the restless spirit was that of a former resident who'd died in the house some years back. Teachers venturing out to mountain-area schools might be well to check into the house they're offered. If they find the frame of a grandfather clock in the place, they might do better to search for accommodation farther afield.

Chapter 4

GHOSTLY
ENCOUNTERS

Ghosts can show up anywhere, on almost any occasion. And sometimes you might not even realize that you are seeing a ghost until it does something unexpected, such as disappearing in front of your very eyes. Keep your wits about you as go about your work and play in the Rocky Mountains, and you may have your own tales of ghostly encounters to relate.

Mountainside Spirits

This Rocky Mountain ghost story takes place in a town named after the Great Spirit, Manitou.

In the early evening of what had been a beautiful summer's day in 1890, the body of Emma Crawford was lowered into a grave on the top of Red Mountain, near Manitou Springs, which is just west of Colorado Springs. The location of the young woman's grave had not been chosen randomly but, rather, was the place of eternal rest that Emma had specifically requested.

Emma's story, both before and after her death from tuberculosis, is a fascinating one. She was engaged to marry a man named Hildebrand when she was taken ill. In keeping with the medical knowledge of that era, her mother took her to the mountains to live. Exposure to mountain air was thought to promote recovery from lung diseases.

For a while it looked as though either the treatment had proven to be effective or that a natural healing process had taken place, for young Emma's condition improved markedly. Heartened by this turn of events, Emma and her intended began to discuss possible dates for the long-postponed wedding to take place.

Naturally, everyone was pleased with the evident improvement in the young woman's health. In addition, Emma's mother and fiancé were also relieved. They'd been increasingly concerned over the effect that Emma's confinement was having upon her personality. The once-outgoing woman had begun to display signs of losing her bubbly personality and becoming somewhat introverted. To put it less delicately, Mr. Hildebrand and Mrs. Crawford both thought Emma had become rather odd over the period of her convalescence.

This assessment, it should be understood, was set against circumstances that might well be considered "odd" in their own right. You see, Mrs. Crawford and Emma, like many people at that time, were spiritualists. They regularly gathered with like-minded people to either host or attend seances. As well, Emma and her mother were both convinced that they each had a specific spirit guide in their lives.

During her recuperation, Emma was not strong and was allowed only limited exercise. Despite these restrictions, one afternoon when her mother was distracted with other obligations, Emma left the house and climbed nearby Red Mountain. She returned from her adventure flushed with exertion and excitement. Mrs. Crawford tried to chastise her daughter but the younger woman explained that she'd had to make the pilgrimage: she'd seen her spirit guide on the slope and he had beckoned to her.

No one in town believed that Emma could have accomplished such an arduous climb, given her fragile health. She assured everyone that she had indeed been up the mountain and, if anyone cared to doubt her, they had only to make the climb themselves and look for the scarf that she'd tied to a pine tree on the mountain's summit.

The next day, a youngster named Bill Crosby and his chum climbed up to the top of Red Mountain. There, just as she'd said, was Emma Crawford's scarf, fluttering from a branch on the pine tree. The ailing young woman who'd rarely left the confines of her home's front yard had, in fact, climbed a mountain.

Unfortunately, it was soon clear that the feat was not a representation of improving health—either mental or physical. Emma began to long for her spirit guide's company again. She maintained that the phantom was a handsome Native man and began to refer to him as her lover.

Not long after her climb, and just a few days before she was to marry Mr. Hildebrand, Emma Crawford's health took a serious turn for the worse. As she lay on her death bed, the bride-to-be uttered her last request. She asked to be buried at the summit of the mountain, under the pine tree that she'd tied her scarf to. This way, she felt, she'd be with her Native lover into eternity.

Those in authority granted her dying wish as best they could. Although they could not get legal permission to do so, they nevertheless trudged up the side of the mountain with the casket containing Emma Crawford's body and buried her remains in the designated spot.

Not long after Emma's funeral, some of the spiritualists in town were hiking Red Mountain when they had an amazing experience. Upon reaching the summit, they stood in awe as they watched a misty figure hovering near Emma's grave. Word spread quickly through the community of believers and the uphill expedition became a popular one. Many people saw the young woman's spirit, and some even saw a second manifestation—that of a handsome young Native American brave.

Charlie's Bowl

Charlie Dupre was a popular skier in the west-central Alberta mountain town of Jasper. It seemed that to know Charlie was to like him. Even today, people remember the young man with warmth and affection. Aside from his charisma, Charlie Dupre's most notable quality was his love of the slopes—he lived to ski. On March 11, 1956, the personable athlete took his last run. He died failing to outrun a deadly avalanche.

Eight years later, an area of Marmot Basin, a well-known ski area near Jasper, was christened "Charlie's Bowl" in recognition of the deceased and his love of skiing. Soon after the honor had been bestowed, workers on the hill began reporting decidedly strange goings-on. Pranks were definitely being played, but no one ever saw the prankster. In addition, no one could figure out why a person would go to all the trouble of being on the slopes at the time that the phantom tricks were being performed, which was in the wee hours of the morning. Eventually, someone recognized the nature of the practical jokes and realized that Charlie Dupre's spirit was haunting the hill.

Art Mulhern, who was in charge of security at the hill, told a journalist that, for the most part, the ghost's antics were innocent and seemed designed only to draw attention to his presence. He did admit that some of the phantom's stunts could become unnerving, especially the ones performed when employees were alone at the lodge after dark.

The snowmaker, who was operating equipment on the hill, was shocked to hear a telephone ring. The switchboard had been closed for hours and he was the only person there, he thought. Despite this knowledge, the man ran to answer the phone. When he picked up the receiver, he found the line dead—just as it should have been when the phones had been turned off for the night. However, he knew that he'd heard that very distinctive sound and he also knew that it had come from the inside of the building. Puzzled, he returned to his snowmaking machine— which was now turned to a different angle than when he had left it. He soon realized that the phantom phone call had merely been a ruse and that now he too had been the object of one of the resident ghost's practical jokes.

The entity is also active inside the lodge. Bottles and dishes that are stored on shelves will, for no apparent reason, be found neatly arrayed—on the floor. Such movements occur when no one—no one visible, that is—has been in these areas of the building. The only clue to this mystery lies in the room's door. It will open and then re-close—without apparent cause.

Charlie's manifestation may also wander from the Marmot Basin area occasionally. Marcella Robe of Alberta believes that she had an encounter with the spirit during a trip to Vernon, in the Interior of British Columbia. She had missed her bus connection just outside Jasper National Park. The cool of evening was coming on and the woman was becoming cold waiting at the side of the road. She headed toward the shelter of a motel complex that she'd noticed not far from the highway. Much to the woman's surprise, a man shuffled past her. Hoping that he might know about the bus schedules in the area, Marcella spoke to him but received no reply. Perhaps he hadn't heard her, the woman thought, and hurried to catch up with the stranger.

"Please, could you tell me the bus schedule?" she inquired again, sure this time that he'd both seen her and heard her question. Once more, the young stranger ignored not only the query but even Marcella's presence. By now she sensed that something was not right. Perhaps the man needed assistance himself.

"What is your name?" she probed.

The first word that the man spoke was clear—"Charlie," he said. The word that followed wasn't as clear, although Marcella explained that what she heard sounded like "Dup ... something."

With that, the image walked past her and into the kitchen area of the motel complex. Marcella watched in amazement as he progressed through the room. No one in the crowded dining room—not customers nor staff—as much as looked up. It was as if the man was invisible to them. Puzzled as she was, Marcella couldn't let the strange encounter distract her from solving her own dilemma. She approached a motel employee, explained her predicament and asked for bus schedule information.

After receiving the help she needed, Marcella's thoughts returned to the strange man whom she'd seen just moments before. Thinking that he too was a lost traveler, she asked the desk clerk if the man had made inquiries.

"What man?" came the puzzled reply.

"Why, the man who just walked through here into the kitchen. Didn't you see a man walk by?" she asked incredulously.

"No," he responded, with a tone of finality that didn't invite further questions.

Completely confused by now, Marcella used the phone at the motel to contact concerned relatives and make travel arrangements. When she was finally reunited with her family, she didn't mention her experience with the strange man that only she seemed to be able to see.

"I could not even explain being stranded, never mind an encounter with a ghost," Robe declared. To this day, the woman remains convinced that the apparition was that of the long-deceased skier, Charlie Dupre.

The Eternal Bride

This poignant legend of a ghostly bride has been haunting Glendale, Wyoming, for at least one hundred years.

Until her wedding day, the girl who was to become this sadly enduring specter led a happy and even privileged life. Her father was a wealthy man and was delighted when a particular young gentleman asked for his daughter's hand in marriage. A date for the wedding was set and that morning the bride and her family prepared with great care. Her white satin gown was as beautiful as anyone in town had ever seen.

The groom and his attendants were expected to arrive from nearby Canon City just before the ceremony was scheduled to start. When he and his friends did not show up on time, the atmosphere of joyful anticipation turned to fearful concern. A party of men rode out to see if they could spot any trouble that might account for the delay.

Not too far out of town, they came to the sight that they'd most hoped they wouldn't encounter—the groom's horse standing beside his lifeless body. The man had been robbed and killed, presumably by those who were ostensibly escorting him to his bride. The search party returned to Glendale to break the tragic news to the young woman and her family.

What was supposed to be a wedding had been replaced by a funeral. Sadder still, just weeks later, there was a second funeral; despite her youth and previous good health, the prospective bride herself had died. Her spirit, however, has apparently endured. Over the years, people traveling through Glendale have reported seeing a slightly transparent image in a white satin bridal gown and veil. Some claim to have heard her call out her lover's name. Others say that they've even heard a ghostly sob. Then, in the blink of an eye, the sight and the sounds have vanished.

The Hermit Haunts

For many years, the banks of the Salmon River in Idaho were haunted by the ghost of a hermit. During his lifetime, the miners at the nearby camp called him "the Mad Monk" because of his peculiar mode of dressing: he wore a hooded burlap robe, tied at the waist. No one knew where he came from or who he was. It seemed that he'd always been there. The miners enjoyed his eccentricities, the children were terrified by them and the Mad Monk himself seemed to enjoy his role as the token mad man in the loosely knit community.

One day, while performing a ritual he apparently took great pleasure in—chasing children away from the riverside shack that he called home—the Mad Monk slipped, fell into the river and was never seen—alive—again. His distinctive robe was found floating in the water some days later.

Everyone was saddened by the loss of their unusual neighbor, and they presumed that they'd heard the last of him. Not so. The Mad Monk, or at least his ghost, turned up in the nearby town of Yankee Fork, where he continued to delight in chasing children. He was also seen walking along the riverbank near the spot where he drowned. In either place, the image would simply vanish if anyone approached him.

The Angry Apparition

When Edward Bainbridge arrived from Scotland in 1866, he was as objectionable a man as Denver, Colorado, had ever had the privilege of hosting. He worked in the Griffith Mountain Mine by day and gambled, cheated and stole by night. Until Wednesday, April 24, 1867, that was pretty well the pattern of Bainbridge's life. That evening he shot and killed a man during a poker game.

Bainbridge fled town immediately but was hunted down by a posse of men who felt nothing but ill will toward the murderer. They caught up with him quickly, arrested him even more quickly and, without wasting time on a trial, hanged him. No sooner had the irascible Scot's neck snapped and his heart beat its last, than his viciously angry spirit showed up back in Denver.

The man's ghost raged about destroying property. At first, the skeptics tried to blame the weather for the cupboard doors that were banging and the lanterns that blew out when no one was near them. Some folks might actually even have been able to believe that it was indeed the wind that was responsible—if it hadn't been for the hauntingly familiar mirthless laughter that accompanied the chaos.

Eventually, the dead man's energy dissipated and town life returned to normal. There was one last report of a sighting. On April 24, 1887, exactly twenty years after Bainbridge had murdered and then himself been murdered, a teenaged girl in

Denver reported seeing the transparent image of an apparition matching the description of the long-dead criminal.

A Headless Horseman

The year 1863 was a frightening time to be in the Colorado area of the Rocky Mountains. A killer, and possibly more than one, was on a rampage. The body count, concern and reward money were all growing. By the time the bounty hit an unprecedented $1500, its purpose was accomplished. The killers were identified as the Espinosa brothers and a posse of vigilantes set out on their murderous trail.

Days later, one of the criminals lay dead but the other had escaped. He didn't stay alone for long but recruited his nephew to take the dead man's place. The newly formed duo ravaged their way through the mountainous countryside, robbing and murdering as they saw fit.

This pair was obviously very dangerous, but the bounty of $1500 was enough to convince at least one man, Tom Tobins, that he could capture the killers. He set off with equal amounts of determination and ammunition. Days later, he proudly rode back into town. Hidden away in a gunny sack astride his mount was the skull of the surviving Espinosa brother.

History has not recorded how, or even if, Tobins spent his reward. One hopes that he lived a long and comfortable life. One also hopes that he was never haunted by Espinosa's headless ghost, for the gruesome-looking specter began appearing to other people as early as 1865.

On a fine summer's day in 1869, a gentleman named Charles Streeter was heading home. He'd reached a point on the route near where Tobins had caught up with and killed the hunted man. There, up ahead on the trail a piece, he saw a strange image—an immobile horse and rider. As he got closer, Streeter realized that there before him was a headless man sitting astride a pure black horse—a sight that he would never forget. Worse, the figure was aiming a firearm his way. Streeter fled. And so did Ramon Costa and Juan Sales when, in 1874, they saw the same manifestation in exactly the same spot.

By the next year, the strength of the vengeful phantom had apparently increased, for it was no longer content just to look threatening. Lieutenant Wilson T. Hartz reported he had actually been pursued by the headless, gun-toting horseman.

Later that same year, two friends, Phillip McKay and Thomas Hatchwood, businessmen from Denver, were riding through the haunted area. By this time, the legend of the frightening specter was well known in the area. McKay and Hatchwood were highly skeptical that such a phenomena could exist and so they rode along in mistaken confidence—until they caught a glimpse of a tall, thin rider on a black horse. The image was lifelike and solid—but it stopped at chest level. It was then that they realized they were staring at the perilous ghost that people spoke of. They rode off in the opposite direction as fast as their horses' legs could take them. Espinosa's ghost initially gave chase but, much to their relief, soon vanished from sight.

It is said that the angry phantom still presides over the area where Espinosa was killed.

An Enduring Entity

The trail through Dead Man's Canyon, roughly ten miles (about fifteen kilometers) south of Colorado Springs, has been haunted by a most unpleasant ghost for well over one hundred years.

It seems that in 1863 the local sawmill owner, William Harkins, was murdered by a group of religious fanatics who, after putting an ax through his skull, also stole his treasured white horse. Some later sightings of Harkins's spirit indicate that he and his horse were reunited in the hereafter; in other sightings his apparition appears alone.

One report of this frightening manifestation occurred in July of 1884 as Mrs. Clark Wyatt, accompanied by her grandson,

This canyon is typical of the type of terrain that our impressions of apparitions have to contend with.

drove her one-horse buggy through the canyon. The sudden appearance of Harkins's ghost startled them both, especially the child. Understandably angered, the woman scolded the image, which apparently responded simply by disappearing.

Mrs. Wyatt was either fortunate or convincing, because Harkins's ghost is usually considerably more persistent. Just twenty years before, a series of big, tough mule-skinners and bull-whackers routinely told hair-raising tales of being pursued through the canyon by a terrible-looking phantom with an ax impaled in its head. Sometimes he was mounted on a white steed, sometimes it was just the horse alone that chased them. No matter how fast they traveled in an attempt to get away from the supernatural presence, it stayed right with them—occasionally tormenting the poor men for up to twenty miles (thirty kilometers).

The ghosts of the man and the horse are, however, credited with once having helped to resolve a tragic mystery. It seems that in 1867, in an eastern state, a young woman was engaged to marry a man named Oliver Kimball. In order to scout out an appropriate place for himself and his intended to settle down, Kimball had headed west. When weeks passed and she hadn't heard from the young man, his bride-to-be sent a note to a Captain Felch in Denver.

The worried woman was, of course, able to offer a detailed description of her fiancé and also, from a letter that he'd sent her, an almost as detailed description of the area that he'd last been in. Felch recognized the description immediately as referring to Dead Man's Canyon and set out to track down the missing man. Not long after he started his search, Felch spotted the phantom white horse off in the distance. The mount was riderless and initially motionless, but it soon turned and led Felch to a dilapidated old cabin where an apparition, thought to be that of William Harkins, climbed onto the steed and rode off up the canyon trail. Felch followed and, at the point where both rider and horse disappeared, he found the remains of Oliver Kimball.

No one ever learned what had caused the young man's death but the ghosts had, at least, spared the young fiancée any further waiting for her betrothed to return.

A Trapline Sighting

Throughout the foothills and valleys of the mountains, the hunting has always been bountiful. For this reason, at one time there were literally thousands of traplines criss-crossing the terrain, interspersed by hundreds of completely isolated trappers' cabins.

During the winter of 1933–34, Gordon Sculthorpe was a twenty-five-year-old trapper. It was his first experience away from his family and he was dreadfully lonely the entire time. One night in January, Sculthorpe was more than lonely. He was frightened as well, for something had wakened him out of a sound sleep. Startled, he propped himself up on one elbow and looked around his one-room cabin. There, much to his surprise, stood his grandmother. The young man stared, uncomprehendingly, at the impossible image for a few seconds—until it vanished before his eyes.

When spring came, Sculthorpe was grateful to get back to civilization. He was saddened, although not surprised, to learn that his grandmother had died one night that past January.

Chapter 5

GHOSTLY GHOST TOWNS

Most so-called ghost towns are not haunted, although verification of this theory is difficult since, by definition, no one is available to report on the presence (or absence) of local ghosts. Thankfully for ghost lovers everywhere, there are some exceptions to this generalization.

Bankhead

Bankhead, Alberta, in Banff National Park, has been a ghost town for nearly eighty years, but it might still be home to a spirit or two. In the early 1900s, it was a bustling, self-sufficient and productive coal-mining community—home to some twelve hundred souls. By the 1920s, the cost of mining the coal had exceeded the mineral's worth and the operation was shut down.

The residential section of the town of Bankhead, as it looked in 1907.

Bankhead, Alberta, once a thriving mining community in the mountains, is now a ghost town. Has it finally been deserted even by its last ghost?

Bankhead's human population dwindled as the mining equipment was moved on to other operations. Many of the houses were also removed and, if you know what to look for, a few of those homes can be seen today in the nearby towns of Banff and Canmore. Inevitably, much was also left behind and some ruins remain still. In one case, something that was left behind has even thrived: you can still harvest rhubarb stalks descended from crops planted by the segregated early-1900s community of Chinese mine workers.

Ruins of the mining buildings also remain at the old townsite and have been incorporated by Parks Canada into something of an outdoor museum. A stroll through the remains and displays is an effective step back into history. Perhaps the spirits of the folks who used to live and work here, now departed, are nearer than one might think, for it takes almost no imagination at all to picture Bankhead's workers and their families going about their daily lives.

All that remains of the church in Bankhead are these stairs and foundation walls.

An article in the September 8, 1934, edition of the *Calgary Albertan* serves to confirm those remaining presences. One of the sub-headlines reads in part, "Caretaker Frightens Away 'a Hundred Ghosts' a Day." The article states, "Some [ghosts] are still left though, for even in broad daylight in any of the empty houses an eerie rapp-rapping goes on in the walls."

The write-up closes with a further hint of remaining entities: "Perhaps the superstitions of the mining folk will hover there to disturb prying antiquarians; there may still be watching spirits ...."

Barkerville

Like Bankhead, Barkerville, British Columbia, is a preserved ghost town where visitors can meander through the streets of history. Although Barkerville is actually a little to the west of the Rocky Mountains, I've included its stories in this book because the haunted history of the place is in much the same spirit as many abandoned Rocky Mountain mining towns.

Compared to Bankhead, in Barkerville even more of the old town remains standing and is therefore available to be explored. For the ghost hunter, it also means that there are more haunted buildings to investigate.

In common with many of the western towns that sprang up in the 1800s to serve the needs of those chasing instant wealth in the gold rush, Barkerville's history is intriguing. In the mid-1800s, Billy Barker, an English sailor, jumped ship and made his way to the Interior of British Columbia. There, along with hundreds of others, he searched for the golden mother-lode. Unlike many others, Billy Barker did strike it rich. As a matter of fact, he found a great deal of gold and became wealthy beyond his wildest imaginings.

Barkerville sprang up, just south and east of Prince George, to supply Barker and the other miners in the area. The town flourished for a number of years and was known far and wide as one of the most law-abiding towns in the West. Such peaceful-ness was not a result of the citizens' inherent goodness, but simply the town's inaccessible location. Barkerville is so out of the way that if a crime was committed, all that was necessary to corner the perpetrator was to seal off the few roads leading out of town. As a result, Barkerville wasn't nearly as rowdy a place as most mining towns. Despite its placid past, Barkerville was haunted already even when it was a burgeoning community.

Today, it is still home to at least three ghosts. But it was a ghostly appearance during the town's heyday that was the most remarkable manifestation. Wellington Moses operated Barker-ville's barber shop. With very little effort beyond opening the shop, he created a successful business and became friendly with many of his customers—including Morgan Blessing, a wealthy and flamboyant American. Blessing had not been raised with money and thus liked to show off what he had acquired, so he wore distinctive gold jewelry made from nuggets that he had mined.

In no time at all, Blessing and Moses became fast friends. Soon they met a third man, James Barry, an unscrupulous fellow who saw the friendship between Moses and Blessing as an opportunity to enrich his own pocketbook. Barry planned on, and succeeded in, causing conflict between the two friends. Soon tensions ran so high that, on their way back from a trip to the coast, Moses left the other two and went on ahead.

Not long after the barber had settled back into his home and shop in Barkerville, he heard that James Barry was also back in town. Morgan Blessing, however, was not. Interestingly, Barry's personal wealth had grown astronomically in just a few short days. Wellington Moses was deeply concerned by this turn of events but, beyond his own suspicions, there was no evidence that anything illegal had occurred. After all, Morgan Blessing was an adult; if he'd decided to move on to another town, rather than return to Barkerville, it was really no one's business but his own. By the same token, James Barry might have come by his new wealth honestly. There was no evidence to the contrary— so far.

Several weeks later, Moses was shocked to see his old friend Morgan Blessing struggling in through the front door of his barber shop. The man looked much the worse for wear. His clothes were ripped and muddy, his complexion pasty, his eyes bloodshot. Barely able to make his way to the barber chair, Blessing indicated to Moses that he wanted a shave.

Speechless with both relief at seeing Blessing again, and concern for the man's obvious distress, Moses set about preparing to give the man the shave that he'd requested. He wrapped Blessing's face in a warm, moist towel before turning to sharpen the razor that he planned to use. When, just a few seconds later, Wellington Moses glanced back at his friend, he saw a sight that he'd never forget—the towel that he'd placed on his friend's face was soaked with blood. Seconds later the man's image vanished. Only the bloodstained towel remained. To Moses, it was clear evidence that a foul and fatal deed had been committed and needed to be avenged. Despite this apparent plea from beyond the grave, there was little that Moses could do to prove that James Barry had murdered and robbed Morgan Blessing.

Several weeks later, Blessing's remains were found, with a single bullet hole in the back of his head. It was now clear that he had been murdered. But the body alone did nothing to implicate James Barry in any way. Barry's connection with the crime went unproven until a Barkerville woman began showing off an unusual pin, explaining that Barry had given it to her. By the middle of the following summer, James Barry had been accused, tried, found guilty of murder and hanged.

Presumably Morgan Blessing's spirit found solace in this justice, for his ghost was never seen in Barkerville again.

Had Mr. Blessing cared to drop in on Barkerville a second time after his death, he would not have been lonely for, even today, there are ghosts in the town. Madame Fannie Bendixon still looks out a second-floor window of the building that housed her saloon. The image is so lifelike that visitors assume that the manifestation is one of the site's historic interpreters. Not so. There is never any living person on the second floor of the old

Inside the 1869 theater in Barkerville, just prior to its closing in 1937.

building because, since the staircase collapsed many years ago, there is no way to get to that level. From descriptions of the oft-seen apparition and records of Fannie Bendixon's appearance, it is clear that the woman's spirit has stayed behind to keep a watchful eye on what was once her business.

Another haunted building in Barkerville is much more puzzling. Barkerville's Theatre Royal of today is not an original building but merely a replica. Despite this lack of authentic history, the place is definitely home to ghosts. Footfalls are routinely heard making their way across the stage floor, when no one can be seen anywhere near that area. Furthermore, isolated pockets of cold air, which are generally acknowledged as indicative of the presence of a spirit in a building, have been noted throughout the theater.

Music has been heard coming from the theater's speakers—even when no power was connected to them—and, during productions in the theater, apparitions have turned up on the stage, especially frequently at stage left. That's where performers report seeing the image of a man, dressed in formal attire from the nineteenth century. In the split second that it takes the startled people to realize that there shouldn't be anyone in that location, the image vanishes. Over the years, that particular ghost's appearance has been reported with amazing consistency. He's described by all who've seen him as sporting a top hat, tails and a mustache. No one knows who the long-deceased dandy might be—just that when he's seen, he's always in the same location and attire. Perhaps before and after he makes his appearances to the living, he relaxes with Fannie at the saloon.

And so, among ghost towns, Barkerville is something of an exception in that more than just the buildings have been preserved—even the spirit of the place lives on.

Bannack

Just about the time that Billy Barker was founding the peaceful little town of Barkerville, Bannack, Montana— or "Grasshopper Diggings," as it was known then—was as rowdy and corrupt a place as you were likely to find anywhere. It's not much wonder that there was so little respect for the law around Bannack: the sheriff was none other than outlaw gang leader Henry Plummer.

Despite this dramatic and traumatic past, the ghost town of Bannack seems only to be haunted by the forlorn cries of babies. The heart-wrenching sounds come from a cabin located in the southeast quadrant of Bannack—a building where, it is generally believed, between eight and fourteen small children died.

Bannack, Montana, where every building has at least one tale to tell.

The Hotel Mead in Bannack, Montana. The ghostly cries of long-deceased babies still echo nearby.

This building housed Skinner's Saloon—a very lively place during Bannack's rough-and-tumble days.

Oddly, Henry Plummer, his gang of "Road Agents" and all the others with whom he was involved have apparently gone on peacefully to their eternal rest.

Ghost Lights in the Cemetery

Silver City, Colorado, is now a ghost town but, even when it was a bustling hive of enterprise, its cemetery was already haunted.

Ghost lights, *ignes faatui*, earth lights, foolish fire, will-o'-the-wisp—by any and all of their many names—are luminous balls of phantom light. They have been seen in almost every imaginable geographic situation—from mountains to prairies and everywhere in between. This oddity is particularly prevalent in cemeteries, and the deserted graveyard in the equally deserted Silver City has provided excellent examples of this enduring and ubiquitous phenomena for nearly two hundred years.

Blue globes of phantom light were noted dancing around the granite cemetery monuments in the town's heyday and, since then, at least once a decade.

Dancing blue ghost lights are also still frequently seen in Silver-Cliff Cemetery, just east of Westcliffe, Colorado. The first documented report of the paranormal phenomenon came in

Cemeteries, such as this one, are often haunted by the souls of the people buried in them.

1890. As the graveyard is the final resting place for many legendary Rocky Mountain characters, it is difficult to speculate as to whose spirit is causing these manifestations of ghostly energy.

Big Sandy Creek

Somewhere along Big Sandy Creek (also known as Sand Creek), just north and west of Denver, Colorado, there is a place that is not a ghost town in the usual sense of the term. For this reason it is, perhaps, even more tragically entrancing.

At dawn, November 29, 1864, during a time of great tension between Native Americans and westward-expanding non-Natives, Colonel John M. Chivington and his some seven or eight hundred men arrived at Big Sandy Creek, where there was a large Native encampment of Cheyenne and Arapaho. If their mission was to kill many of the inhabitants (and there has been much controversy as to what really happened and why), then they were successful, for that is precisely what they proceeded to do.

Despite several government investigations, no one was ever punished for the massacre. Possibly because of this lack of justice, the ghosts of the casualties continue to haunt the area. But, it is not just that the spirits of the fallen that are seen and heard. Even their temporary town, as it existed the day of the killings, is also seen.

Almost exactly a year after the shameful incident, a buffalo hunter reported seeing a group of Cheyenne camped out on the shores of Big Sandy Creek. He sent a scout to speak to the group, but by the time the man got to the point where the encampment had been seen, no one was there; nor was there any clue that anything or anyone had been there recently. Although he saw nothing, the scout sensed a great deal, and none of those feelings were good. He experienced sensations that indicated to him that great anguish had been suffered on that spot.

Even though he could not argue with what his scout had— or, more accurately, had not—found, the hunter insisted that he'd seen a populated village. Worse, that sighting was not the only one that appeared to the man. Eleven months later, he stared in disbelief at a similar scene in the same area. This second time, however, he also heard melancholy chanting.

Once the phantom town became known, people would make a point to stop at the curve in Big Sandy Creek where the sightings had occurred to see if they too could experience retrocognition—

seeing that which has previously existed but is no longer there. In 1896 and again in 1902, photographers tried to capture the spectral image on film, but they were not successful.

A woman who happened upon the site in 1911 searched the area for hours looking for the source of the crying that she clearly heard. In 1956, another woman, someone who had no idea of the area's history, happened to arrive at the haunted spot. Although she did not see anything, she was suddenly and inexplicably overcome with feelings of terror and grief.

It can easily be argued that the phantom Native American settlement on the shores of Big Sandy Creek is a ghost town in a true sense.

Chapter 6

THE SPIRIT'S INN

While you are traveling, a hotel room often serves as your home-away-from-home. It shouldn't be too surprising then, that, like haunted houses, many of these temporary lodgings have resident ghosts.

As the next few stories demonstrate, like ghosts anywhere, these hostelry-based spirits can range from being barely noticeable to being a terrible nuisance.

The Spirit of Skoki Lodge

When he was alive, Christopher Paley, or "Kit," as he was sometimes called, was a widely respected mathematician. In the 1930s, Paley and his friends came from their homes in the United States to ski in the Canadian Rockies. Sadly, it was the combination of Paley's genius and the snow conditions one day that resulted in tragedy. The man was distracted by a mathematical problem that he had been attempting to solve and, in order to gain solitude and ponder the troubling equation without interruption, he repeatedly skied away from his friends.

His companions were well used to Paley's occasional need to be alone and, under safer circumstances, would have respected it. This time his desire for solitude could not be ignored, for he was putting his life in peril by skiing into areas at risk of avalanche. Despite their efforts, Kit Paley's friends were not successful in controlling where the distracted man skied, and he died that day, buried by torrents of cascading snow. Since that tragic moment, Christopher Paley's ghost has not left the Ptarmigan Valley in west-central Alberta.

To this day, skiers have described having seen lights on in Skoki Lodge, the little building where Paley and his friends had stayed, and smoke coming from the chimney. When they approached the cabin, however, they were confused to find it cold, empty and dark, even though, just moments before, it had shown distinct signs of welcoming life inside.

At other times, people have reported watching a skier appear suddenly, out of nowhere—only to disappear equally suddenly. In addition to the mysterious appearance, followed by the even more confusing vanishing act, witnesses often attest to having seen the phantom's fluorescent skis trailed by glowing flames.

In 1993, while in Lethbridge to do readings from my first collection of ghost stories, I was approached by a teenaged girl who had been raised with the legend of Christopher Paley. It seems that, as a youngster, her mother had been skiing in the area of Skoki Lodge. She'd apparently been enjoying herself so much that she hadn't paid much attention to either the time or the rapidly diminishing daylight. Unfortunately, by the time that she did notice, she was quite a distance from the safety of her cabin. Quite frightened, she headed in what she hoped was the right direction. Suddenly, a figure skied out from a stand of trees and came along beside, but slightly behind, her. Although she never saw the presence clearly, she knew that she was no longer alone. The specter stayed with her until they came within sight of the little lodge before vanishing as quickly as it had appeared.

The young woman relating her story to me had a very personal reason to be grateful to a man who'd lived and died many years before she had been born. If it hadn't been for the ghost of Christopher Paley, the woman who was to become her mother might well have died before reaching adulthood.

As a tribute and an explanation for the mathematician's continuing presence on the slope, poet John Porter crafted *The Legend of the Halfway House*. In the work, he describes Paley's possible arrival at the Pearly Gates, his lack of interest in heaven's ski slopes, and his spirit's subsequent return, for eternity, to the best place on earth to ski.

Ten Thousand Frights

Just out of Santa Fe, New Mexico, is an unlikely spot in which to find a Japanese-style health spa, but the Ten Thousand Waves is just exactly that. More interesting still is that there's a ghost story associated with its history.

A man named Duke Klauch bought the place in the 1980s and began to notice paranormal encounters almost immediately. At the most inconvenient hour of 3 AM, Klauch reported hearing what sounded to him like metal chains being dragged across the floors. Although he investigated each occurrence immediately and thoroughly, he was never able to discover a source for the upsetting noises.

The new owner had no clue as to what might be the possible cause for these sounds until the woman from whom he had bought the place paid him a call. She asked Klauch, point-blank, if he'd seen her daughter anywhere on the premises. Klauch was shocked at such a question, as he hadn't even known that the woman had a daughter, let alone that she might somehow have stayed behind or returned.

In answer to his puzzlement, she revealed that her daughter was no longer alive. During a party held at the house, she explained, the youngster had become terribly upset and had killed herself. The child's remains had been buried on the property. The location had likely been disturbed by Klauch's renovations to the landscape, causing the girl's spirit to become temporarily active—and doubtless she was responsible for the nocturnal racket.

A worker whom Klauch had hired for the early morning shift regularly heard phantom footfalls on a staircase. The sounds moved from the front door and along the hallway till they reached the area where the worker stood. Thinking that possibly someone had come into the building, the worker checked the locks. All were securely bolted. Nevertheless, the man knew what he'd heard, so he searched the premises thoroughly but always determined that he was indeed alone.

Just as he was beginning to accept that this supernatural activity was not a cause for alarm, another sound was added to the ghostly cacophony—the sound of a door slamming. The spirit's strength was apparently growing. It wasn't too many days after he first heard that sound that he finally saw the apparition.

He felt her presence before he actually saw her and, when she did manifest, it was as a still, white mist that remained visible for a while before disappearing before his eyes. The man told Klauch of his experience and it was determined that they should call in an expert.

Toward that end, three priests came out to the Ten Thousand Waves spa and walked from room to room blessing the place, reading passages from the Bible and sprinkling the entire inside of the building liberally with holy water. Just before the trio left, they hung a crucifix on the wall. Since then, there have not been any specters seen, heard or felt at the resort—with one exception. A cleaner once unthinkingly removed the cross from its usual spot. Immediately the ghostly sounds began to manifest once again. The religious symbol was rehung and the place has been phantom-free ever since.

The Black Cat Guest Ranch

The Black Cat Guest Ranch is nestled in the first range of Rockies foothills, just west of Hinton, Alberta. The ranch is a rustic retreat that welcomes groups as well as individual bookings. In 1992, while the ranch was hosting a writers' retreat, a severe storm thundered in. As if to create a dramatic setting for the great novel that all the wordsmiths probably hoped that they'd craft, the electricity went out. Rather than putting pen to paper, however, the writers spent the evening huddled together in the main room of the ranch, candles providing their only illumination, as they scared each other with ghost stories.

Amber Hayward, part owner of the Black Cat and an accomplished writer herself, was able to add to the intimacy of the moment by relating an incident that had occurred at the ranch when the building where the little group now sat was under construction.

The encounter occurred to Mary Bond, Amber's mother, who, when I called to ask about the tale, was disarmingly matter-of-fact in her retelling.

"It was the summer of 1976 and we were building a new lodge," Mary began. "We had a portable generator for power. One day, I wanted to do dishes, so I needed power [to heat the water], and walked over to the construction site. I looked into the foundation. It was nearly two meters [a little over six feet] deep at that point. There was a big man standing there [in the excavation]. He could not possibly have gotten down there without a ladder, not a man that big."

The only ladder on the property was with Mary's husband and son-in-law, who were at a different part of the site that day.

Part of the charm of the Black Cat Ranch is that it is secluded. With directions, the place is simple enough to find, but it's highly unlikely that anyone would just happen upon that particular location, let alone find it and then jump into a deep construction pit.

Assuming that the man was there to see either her husband or her son-in-law, Mary simply went on about her work. That evening, she asked her husband, "Who was your visitor?"

He replied, "What visitor?"

Mary described the man whom she'd seen that afternoon, but the description meant nothing to her husband. Furthermore, he assured his wife, there hadn't been any man, of any description, visiting the site at any point that day.

Puzzled by the contradiction between what she knew she had seen and her husband's assurances that no one had been there, Mary made a point to return the next day at exactly the same time to the place where she'd seen the man. Although she was well used to the appearance of the excavation, Mary hoped that the second trip would prove that what she'd thought she'd seen had merely been an optical illusion. It proved nothing of the sort.

"There were no shadows," she recalled.

Who, then, could the apparition have been? Of course, there's no way to know for sure, but Mary has a theory that is connected to the history of the area. Local legends tell of Cree braves who once walked from what is now the province of Ontario all the way to the Rocky Mountain foothills, where the Black Cat Ranch is located. Some of those travelers settled in the area, and were eventually buried there, too. Mary Bond believes that the ghost that she saw may have been the image of a member of that group. Perhaps the apparition was merely curious about what Mary's family was doing with the land that he had settled on so many years before, for he has never been seen again.

Room 6 Receives Special Room Service

This story traveled far and wide to end up right back where it belongs—in a book about Rocky Mountain ghosts. The following incident, which occurred in the Alberta mountain-park town of Banff, was reported to the century-old Institute for Psychical

Research in London, England. The name of the hotel where the unexplained event took place has, unfortunately, been lost along the tale's trek. As the lodge is described as being "small, cozy and friendly," we can rule out the larger and more formal hotels in the town.

The story goes that, in the early 1980s, a family named Fourche was touring western Canada. The daughter, Sonya, who was fourteen at the time, had diabetes. Over the years, she'd become accustomed to dealing with her body's special requirements for regular nutrition and added insulin. As a result, with a minimum of assistance, Sonya led a normal, happy and productive life.

As the family checked into hotels across the country, they always arranged for an 8 AM wake-up call for Sonya. No matter how tired the girl was, she needed to be up at that time to eat a nourishing breakfast and take her medication, because her health depended on conscientiously adhering to a strict schedule. The evening that the Fourches arrived in Banff was no exception. As they checked into the hotel, weary from a full day's travel, Sonya's father arranged for the wake-up call to be made to his daughter's room the next morning.

At precisely at 8 AM, the phone in Room 6 rang. The clerk greeted Sonya with a cheery good morning and assured her that breakfast would be at her door in less than five minutes. The young woman barely had time to complete her early morning insulin routine before a delicious meal was delivered to her door. She ate her breakfast and waited for her parents, asleep in the next room, to awaken, and for the day's adventures to begin.

The Fourche family spent the day exploring all they could in Banff National Park. They returned to their hotel exhausted, but pleased with the day. Before retiring to their respective rooms, Sonya and her father reminded the desk clerk of the importance of the next day's wake-up call.

When they were assured that the request had been duly recorded and would most certainly be followed up on, the father and daughter bid each other good night and retired to their separate rooms.

Just as it had the first morning, the ringing of Sonya's phone awakened her the second morning, and, upon answering, she heard a clerk deliver a message almost identical to the one the day before. Surprised at how tired she still felt, the youngster was able to make herself get out of bed only by remembering how good breakfast had been the day before, and by anticipating a similar treat momentarily. She took care of her daily injection and then checked outside her door to see if breakfast had arrived yet. It hadn't, she was disappointed to note, so Sonya decided to get washed. She hurried in the shower so that her breakfast would still be hot when she brought it in from the hallway but, when she opened the door a second time, the meal still hadn't been delivered.

After checking a third and fourth time to see if room service had been there yet, Sonya gave up and went into her parents' bedroom to ask what they thought she should do about the tardy service. Much to her surprise, Sonya's parents were still fast asleep. She wakened her mother, who groggily asked what time it was. Sonya replied that it had to be eight-thirty by now, because the phone call to waken her had come at least half an hour ago.

With that, both Sonya and Mrs. Fourche glanced at the latter's travel alarm clock. The instrument indicated that it was not yet 5 AM. The clock had to be wrong, they decided. The desk clerk wouldn't have made the call more than three hours too early. Sonya returned to her room, where she checked her wristwatch. Sure enough, the time shown by her watch matched what her mother's clock had read. Apparently, someone had called Sonya's room and disturbed her sleep hours before she needed to be awake.

Thinking that a hotel employee had played a rather cruel practical joke, Mrs. Fourche told Sonya that they would deal with the issue after a few more hours of sleep. She suggested that her daughter also try to get back to sleep. Fortunately, the girl's insulin dosage had been regulated successfully for a number of months and so, although the premature injection was not a good thing, it would not cause any harm.

As no one was able to fall back to sleep too soundly, Sonya and her parents were up and dressed before 8 AM. They met in the hallway and decided to deal with the problem at the front desk before they went for breakfast.

Mr. Fourche approached the clerk and reminded him of his obligation to phone Sonya's room. The clerk acknowledged the responsibility and apologized. He explained that he was running two or three minutes behind schedule in making the morning calls. Sonya replied that someone who was more than three hours ahead of schedule had already made the call.

The desk clerk stared uncomprehendingly, and then explained that such an early morning call was an impossibility at that hotel. Not only was the front desk not staffed before eight o'clock in the morning, but the bells on the telephones in the rooms were always turned off throughout the night so that guests would not be disturbed.

For a few seconds, Mr. Fourche and the desk clerk stared at one another over the counter. Neither was pleased with the way that the conversation had gone. Just as Mr. Fourche turned from the front desk in exasperation, the clerk called him back. He'd just remembered that he'd given Sonya Room 6—the haunted room. As best he could, the hotel employee explained that Sonya's experience was not the first incident in that particular room. Judging by similar events in the past, the teenager's early morning wake-up call had been initiated by an overly dedicated employee—one who had been dead for several years.

The clerk produced a notebook from under the counter. He asked the family to record the event alongside reports from other guests who'd stayed in Room 6. Annoyed and somewhat shaken, the Fourches refused the request and checked out of the hotel.

Apparently Mr. Fourche waited until the family vacation was over before contacting the Institute for Psychical Research and telling their experience. The institute immediately contacted the hotel, where the staff not only confirmed the family's story, but eagerly shared the contents of the journal to which the Fourches had refused to contribute.

The Ghosts of Jasper Park Lodge

People travel great distances for the privilege of staying at the Jasper Park Lodge in Alberta. And it's no wonder—nestled in the grandeur of the Canadian Rockies, the lodge really does have it all, including luxurious surroundings and an alert, capable staff to cater to your every need. Oh yes, and it has ghosts too.

Mario Rulli, the sales coordinator for the establishment, explained that most of the paranormal activity at the lodge seems to be done by a former employee believed to haunt the Point Cabin.

"Supposedly, in the late '40s or early '50s, a chambermaid was climbing the stairs [in the Point Cabin] that lead to a small card room. A guest surprised her ... and she fell [to her death]," Mario related. "Since that incident, there have been numerous happenings in the Point Cabin."

One of those "happenings" occurred during the winter in an era when the hotel was open only during the summer.

"There were workers in the cabin doing slight renovations [to] the interior. This involved placing the furniture in the middle of the room. Every morning when they came back to the cabin ... they found the furniture had been moved all about," he said. "A couple of them decided to investigate, anticipating that it was staff fooling around. As they approached the cabin, they noticed that the lights were on, but when they entered, the lights were off. No one was in the cabin. They exited the cabin and decided to hide nearby so that they could catch the prankster. They saw lights turn on and smoke coming out of the chimney."

Showing a remarkable amount of courage, the pair ran inside the cabin again. They found the room dark, with no fire in the fireplace. Worse, the furniture had been rearranged. They looked around for footprints in the snow surrounding the cabin, but found none.

The employees couldn't have been entirely surprised by the situation, because the haunting of the Point Cabin is well known around the lodge. The switchboard has received calls from the cabin, and people have reported seeing lights going on and off—all when the cabin was unoccupied. When the cabin is occupied, the television has been known to develop a mind of its own and change channels by itself.

But the maid in the Point Cabin isn't the only ghost at Jasper Park Lodge. There are also the dining-room ghosts. Apparently these two are an elderly couple who suddenly appear and then just as suddenly disappear.

"The ghosts seem harmless but enjoy watching staff run hysterically out of [the] room," according to Mario Rulli.

Considering the advantages that guests enjoy when staying at Jasper Park Lodge, it shouldn't be too much of a surprise that at least a few spirits have chosen to make this luxurious hotel their very permanent home.

A Haunted Hotel

In June of 1995, I was invited to attend a reception at the Banff Springs Hotel in Alberta to celebrate the completion of an hour-long television special documenting some of the haunted places in western Canada. The event was held in a room off the Rob Roy Dining Room.

The location hadn't been chosen at random: it was near there that, over the years, many hotel employees had reported seeing an apparition of a bride dancing a solitary waltz. The image is widely believed to be the ghost of a bride who died there on her wedding day. She was making her entrance down a spiral staircase when the train of her bridal gown brushed up against one of the candles used to illuminate the stairs. The material caught fire and the young woman panicked and fell to the bottom of the stairs. She died instantly, her neck broken.

Shortly after the tragic accident, the staircase was bricked up. The result was a curving stairway that went up about a dozen steps before ending abruptly at a solid brick wall—a strange sight indeed. When I heard that work crews were tearing down the brick wall, I was curious as to whether this renovation might provoke some additional ghostly activity. Hoping to allow sufficient time for an encounter to occur, I let a couple of months go by before calling the hotel with my inquiry.

The hotel's public relations department was delighted to report that the demolition had revealed a fabulous stone floor that they hadn't previously known about, but that was pretty much all. To date, there had been no further sightings of the slightly transparent dancing bride.

To my knowledge, no one in our group of celebrants that June evening saw the long-deceased bride either, but the location of our gathering provided an additional story. A young woman serving at the party informed me that one particular elevator in the hotel will always return to the ninth floor. That's where Sam McCauley, a former bellman at the hotel, was rumored to have hidden his tips. Janet Plunkett, a long-time co-worker and friend of Sam's, reported that after he died, whenever she was on that floor, she could sense his presence and often heard phantom sounds coming from empty rooms.

"There were a few people who thought he was there," she explained. Clearly, Janet was not the only one to have felt his spirit and heard footsteps, doors closing and water running—all when there was no rational explanation for the noises.

McCauley is still seen helping out around the hotel occasionally—even though he's been dead for fifty years. One couple had an especially dramatic encounter with McCauley's ghost—he actually helped them with their luggage. Another guest checked out in the middle of the night after learning that there was no one employed at the hotel who matched the description of the elderly man in an old-fashioned uniform who had just knocked on her door.

The ghosts of the bride and the bellman are not the only paranormal manifestations to have haunted the Banff Springs

Hotel. One entity that hasn't been seen since 1926 was probably the ghost of an architect involved in the planning of the original hotel. Prior to a devastating fire at this mountain hostelry, security guards would report encountering a shadowy image in a specific area of the building. While cleaning up after the fire, workers noted something of a secret room just next to where the apparition had been reported. It was suspected that the architect had made an error and created a room with no windows or doors, and was so tormented by his mistake in life that he haunted the spot after his death. That ghost has not been seen since the fire.

Legend also has it that disembodied voices have occasionally been heard in different areas of the castle-like structure, and that other specters have been seen around the hotel. The spirits of a deceased bartender, a maid and a bagpiper have been reported.

It is said that Stephen King found his stay at the Banff Springs Hotel so inspiring that it propelled him to write his classic novel, *The Shining*. What a tribute to this wonderfully haunted hostelry!

The Phantom Inn

In the late 1970s, Fred Syska and Andrea, the woman who is now his wife, were driving through the Canadian Rockies as they made their way from Vancouver back to their home in Edmonton, Alberta. The most challenging part of the drive through the mountains was behind them by now and, had it been daylight, they could still have seen those mountains on the western horizon.

They both knew that they were close to home but, despite this proximity to Edmonton, Fred wanted to stop for the night. They'd driven almost nonstop throughout the day and he felt that he was too tired to go any farther safely. He and Andrea were much relieved when, a few minutes after deciding to stop for the night, they saw a roadside motel's illuminated sign just off the highway.

The couple drove into the parking lot and pulled up beside the motel office. The place seemed eerily deserted. The brightly lit sign that had captured their attention from the highway was the only indication of life around the rather run-down looking motel. The office door was closed, but unlocked, and so they walked in, expecting to be greeted by a possibly sleepy owner. Much to their surprise, the place was completely unoccupied.

After looking around for a few confused seconds, the pair noticed a handwritten note on the counter. Presumably written by the motel's proprietors, the message directed guests to leave the room fee of eight dollars in the envelope beside the note and to take a key.

They followed the instructions, but Fred did think that the motel's owners were "remarkably trusting." However, the pair's overall thoughts were of the much-needed rest that this odd little inn could provide for them.

The key that Fred picked up was for Unit 12, so they moved their car from in front of the office down the line of units to the appropriate stall. As they did, they noted that they appeared to be the only guests at the motel that night. There were no other cars in the lot and the doors to all the rooms had been left open at least a crack.

Not knowing whether the strange sensations that they were increasingly feeling came from being so tired or from being in such a strange place, Andrea and Fred entered Unit 12 somewhat hesitantly. Through the bathroom window, Fred could see that there was another, identical row of motel units directly behind them—all obviously vacant.

By now Fred and Andrea's feelings of discomfort were intensifying. Fred was suffering from that terribly unnerving awareness that he was being watched, even though he could see that he and Andrea were alone. Attempting to ignore the growing tension in order to take advantage of the potential rest that the strange place could offer them, Fred began to undress. Soon his level of discomfort had increased to a feeling of foreboding doom, which in turn became a premonition that something terrible might happen if they did fall asleep. As that sensation crystallized, the feeling of being watched strengthened.

Seconds later, they bolted from the room, ran back to the motel office to retrieve their money and drop off the key, and headed for the safety of their car. They drove in silence until they found another, more ordinary, motel—where they spent an uneventful night.

Several days later, they were relating their strange experience to a friend well familiar with that strip of highway. The man was astonished to hear their detailed description of the eerie motel. He passed the spot regularly and was positive that there was no building there at all, let alone a motel with a brightly lit sign. He promised to check the next time he drove that stretch of highway and then report back to the puzzled couple.

Weeks later, true to his word, the man drove past the spot that Fred and Andrea had described as being the location of the motel. Just as he had thought, there was nothing there— no building, merely an empty field. Now very curious, the friend began to make inquiries of people who knew the area even better than he did. One of those he consulted was an officer with the Royal Canadian Mounted Police who'd served in that area for many years. The Mountie was sure that nothing matching that description still existed along the highway. However, a motel meeting the exact specifications of the strange place that Andrea and Fred had found just weeks ago had indeed once existed—but it had been torn down eight or nine years previously.

That August long weekend when they were so exhausted from their drive through the Rockies, Fred and Andrea had briefly checked into a phantom motel.

The Well-haunted Prince of Wales Hotel

Waterton Lakes National Park is the Canadian portion of a Rocky Mountain preserve that straddles the Alberta-Montana border and celebrates the peaceful relationship between Canada and the United States.

The Prince of Wales Hotel in Waterton dates back to the 1920s. When it opened, the price of a night's accommodation was just less than ten dollars. Many people felt that the rate was excessive, but those who could afford it happily paid the price for the privilege of being surrounded by the park's striking geography and pampered by the attentive staff at the luxurious hotel.

Two women, both former employees at the Prince of Wales, have felt such an affinity for the place that they seem to have taken up residence on a permanent basis. To date, one has stayed for over fifty years and the other one for more than twenty.

A construction worker—let's call him "Joe"—was involved in a re-roofing project at the hotel. He had quite a story to tell about his encounters with the older of the two spirits and her influence on the renovations. Part of Joe's responsibilities included taking detailed measurements and assessing what materials would be required to bring each room up to standard. All the rooms that he worked on were on the hotel's west side, but spread from the second to the sixth floors.

"These rooms had been vacant for a number of years, but the proprietors thought they could redo [them] and make them available for guests," Joe explained, and then added, "it was on

This luxurious hotel in Waterton National Park, near the Alberta-Montana border, is said to be home to two female ghosts.

the sixth floor that I first encountered the strangeness that still leaves me baffled."

Joe described the rooms on the sixth floor as being in four groups of four. "I was measuring rooms in the northwest quadrant when I heard a door slam. There was no one else up at that level. The regular maintenance staff was down on level one and the roofers were outside. I didn't think anything about it at the time, attributing the door closure to the wind. The Prince of Wales is an old building and drafty, so a door closing could easily have been [caused] by the wind," Joe assured me.

He finished up where he was and prepared to repeat the process in the next room—the room with the now-closed door.

"Somehow the door had locked upon closing. I had to walk down six levels to find a maintenance person, get keys from him, and walk back up to the sixth. When I got back [to the room] the door was open," Joe reported. "There was no one about. I walked into the room. It was cold, much colder than the adjacent rooms."

By now Joe recognized that he was dealing with extraordinary circumstances. His reactions were intriguing: "It wasn't that I was afraid, but curious, about what was going on. I sat down in the room .... The temperature in [there] got warmer and with it a sense of injustice done in the room permeated my thinking. After I had 'communicated' with the strangeness, I went about my work and left the room."

Still curious about what might have caused his experience, Joe began subtly probing the hotel staff for information. It was then that he heard something about a ghost in the hotel. "Although the reports seemed to indicate that the entity moved about the hotel, for the most part the reports centered around the northwest corner," he told me. Of course that was the area in which Joe had encountered the strangeness that he had described.

"Legend had it that a murder took place up in that area shortly after the Second World War. The upper levels of the hotel [at that time] were given over to staff," he said. "One of the cooks and his wife lived in the area in question. She was a vivacious, outgoing, friendly concierge. He was an extremely jealous person. One Friday night she returned to their room after spending a few hours playing cards with other staff. Her husband, in a fit of rage, killed her."

The husband then fled from the couple's quarters, having locked the door behind himself. Just as he had no doubt hoped, his wife's body was not found until the following Monday. By then, he must have put considerable distance between himself and the corpse, because he was never caught. Joe was told that the hotel staff now believe the banging doors and creaking noises are attempts by the deceased to draw attention to the grievous injustice perpetrated upon her.

While Joe was carrying out his duties inside, other workers were laboring on the roof of the hotel.

"They were [working] on an area of the roof that was over the room in question. This section was proving tougher to get through than the rest. The workers' nails tended to bend and shingles were slipping from their hands. They attributed it to frost, wind and harder than normal wood," Joe explained. "I took a different approach. I went back inside and climbed up the six floors to the room [with the door] that had slammed shut on me. I entered the room and in a calm voice talked to the room. I said that by letting the roofers pound their nails in and hold onto their shingles they would be away from the area quicker and peace should follow. I felt something that I can't describe and [then I] left the room. I returned outside and, when the roofers came down, I asked them how things were going. They said that, for some inexplicable reason, the nails were not being bent and the shingles were not slipping from their grasp. They made record time on that portion of the roof and were on to other sections."

The other spirit at the hotel is Sarah. She's an apparition who is actually still seen occasionally by staff at the Prince of Wales Hotel. As a teenager, Sarah worked at the facility. She apparently had a schoolgirl crush on a fellow employee—an executive with the hotel. Her feelings were not reciprocated and the result was tragic. The youngster jumped to her death from the hotel's seven-story-high bell tower.

One guest whom I spoke with reported that he and his wife could feel, although not see, someone tucking them into their bed on the nights that they stayed there. He also commented that, no matter how many times he opened the window, when he woke up it was closed and locked. The man assured me that he had no history of sleepwalking and that his wife reported sleeping soundly through the night while they were at the hotel. Perhaps Sarah was afraid the guests would be subjected to a draft if the window remained open overnight. The couple added that they felt comforted by what they perceived as the special presence in their room.

The price of accommodation at the Prince of Wales Hotel in Waterton National Park has certainly changed over the years, but you can still count on attentive staff, luxurious amenities, glorious scenery and—as with the past fifty years—a ghost or two.

The Ghost of Henry Hoet's House

The Prince of Wales Hotel might have had one more ghost if Henry Hoet's spirit had not settled into the unusual home that he had lovingly constructed in the foothills town of Cardston, Alberta, just east of the international Waterton-Glacier National Parks. Although he's been dead for many years now, the house is thought to still be home to the master craftsman who built it.

Both Henry Hoet and his house would have been considered oddities no matter where they were or when. In 1911, in the predominantly Mormon town of Cardston, both were considered to be nothing short of objects of fascination. The Mormon

An exterior shot of Henry Hoet's masterpiece of architectural craftsman-ship, which is still home to his spirit.

people place an enormous amount of importance on a person's genealogy. Henry was an intriguing puzzle right from the start, for he seemed to have come out of nowhere when he arrived in their tiny and isolated community. Although he did acknowledge that he'd been born and raised in Belgium, Hoet gave no other indication about his heritage.

He immediately set about renovating and enlarging the small, two-story house that he had purchased in Cardston. The place had been one of the original residences in the town, built in the late 1800s by a pioneer Mormon family. The location of the house, on the bank of Lee's Creek, was considered to be a real drawback to everyone except Henry, for the creek had flooded ten years earlier, leaving exposed cobblestones strewn over most of the property. To Henry, the rocks were a real advantage: it meant a nearly infinite supply of free building materials. Today, the house that he painstakingly created over the years is, because of their use, known as "Cobblestone Manor."

Over the years, the architectural masterpiece has been called by many other names—"the Rock House," "the Wonder House" and even, long before it was actually haunted, "the Ghost House." According to the Flickingers, the home's current owners, and James Musson, who wrote a book about Hoet and his house, by now there's little question that Hoet's benign spirit is in residence there.

Considering the history of the beautiful old house, it's not surprising that Henry's presence has remained as a ghostly legacy. For years, the man labored day in and day out to build the spectacular place. During this time he kept very much to himself but, when he did speak to others in the community, it was often of the woman whom he had left behind in his native land and how he'd soon be sending for her. We can never know whether Henry Hoet actually did have a lady-love who stayed behind in Europe or whether she was merely a figment of his decidedly odd

These intricate wood designs were all built by Henry Hoet as part of the enticement to get his mysterious (and possibly non-existent) lady-love to follow him to Canada from Belgium.

mind. It is known that he never received a letter, let alone a guest, from overseas.

Through it all, Henry worked on crafting his extraordinary dwelling, in an amazing demonstration of his talents. In order to support himself and purchase the expensive materials that he was putting into the house, Hoet hired himself out to help build both the Mormon Temple in Cardston and the (now haunted) Prince of Wales Hotel some distance to the west. As soon as he could, Hoet would return to devote himself to building his home. Nothing short of a masterpiece began to emerge.

In an era when those few homes that were wired for electricity had, at most, a bare bulb hanging from the middle of one room, Hoet's house had, in one room alone, forty handmade light fixtures. "It would have seemed like magic," pronounced author James Musson.

Though he built the exterior walls with the cobblestones that had washed up on his property, he ordered most of the materials for the interior from Europe. For a period of time after each one of those shipments arrived, Henry Hoet's behavior was even more bizarre than it usually was. He would talk to himself and work on his house for days without stopping to either rest or eat.

By 1928, the man's mental health had deteriorated to the point that he was incarcerated. Not long afterward, word spread that he had died. Immediately after that news arrived, rumors began circulating throughout Cardston that the man's spirit had returned, in death, to the fabulous house that he'd crafted in life. Other than this supposed, ethereal occupant, and the odd meeting of a local group of Masons, the house stood vacant for more than twenty years, its reputation as a haunted house increasing with each season. No one wanted to buy the place because they were afraid of the ghost. Ironically, Hoet, the man supposedly haunting it, was actually alive for most of those years. Henry Hoet did not die until the spring of 1949.

A retrospective examination of the facts indicates that it was syphilis that had caused both his mental illness and his eventual death.

In 1977, Ed and Arlene Flickinger bought Cobblestone Manor and, after rebuilding the parts of the place that had deteriorated over the years, opened a restaurant in Hoet's former home. The business has been a complete success, perhaps an indication that the resident phantom approves of both the Flickingers and their use of the property.

Arlene good-naturedly admits that the ghost gets blamed for "everything we've lost and everything else [that goes wrong]," but even so, she firmly believes that the builder has stayed on. As proof, she notes that over the years they've noticed time and time again that lights that they were sure had been turned off were burning brightly, that doors that they were positive had been closed were found standing open.

In James Musson's book he assures readers that Arlene is well aware of Hoet's "quiet and humble spirit" about the place. Musson himself seems to feel that same presence, for he once told a journalist that "a spirit ... inundate[s] the place." That

The stained-glass panels and lamps are trimmed in hand-carved wood. The number of light fixtures in this house may have originally contributed to rumors about the place being possessed.

spirit might also have had a hand in directing the subject of the book that Musson wrote for, when he began his project, he intended that a write-up about Cobblestone Manor would form just a portion of a book about unusual owner-built homes. Despite his best intentions, researching the history of the Cardston house and its original owner soon became an obsession with Musson, one that did not let him rest until he'd written and published an entire book, *Grand Delusions*, devoted to Henry Hoet and Cobblestone Manor.

In the process of researching and writing the book, Musson spent a great deal of time at the unique southern Alberta house, including many quiet, reflective moments in the middle of the night. Although no one's ever seen the spirit of Henry Hoet, James acknowledges, like Arlene, "I can tell you this, when you are up at 2:00 or 3:00 in the morning, sitting in that Dark Oak Room it is an incredible feeling. You don't feel alone but you don't feel threatened either. There seems to be a presence. It's a good serene feeling and a feeling that this man is present, but then I guess one would get that feeling because everything in there ... is saturated with the oils from his fingers. It just oozes his presence. It just oozes throughout. It has captured me."

It would seem that, finally, as a ghost, Henry Hoet has found the peace that evaded him during his life.

Guests of Ghosts

In March of 1989, three friends were driving from eastern Wyoming due south to Denver, Colorado. As will happen in that region at that time, a raging blizzard blew up and the group of travelers decided that it was best to seek shelter until the storm abated. They considered themselves fortunate to spot a restaurant almost immediately, and more fortunate still when they walked in, for they found the place deserted except for two very pleasant waitresses. As they were being seated, the group noted that the menu offerings were tempting; better yet, the food, when it came, was delicious.

The trio's best surprise came after their meal, when the waitress brought them the bill. The total for all three meals was less than ten dollars. The friends thanked the waitresses for their well-served, satisfying meal and, as tangible proof of their appreciation, left a generous tip. By the time that they'd finished eating, the weather had cleared sufficiently that the three felt that they could complete their drive.

The waitress who'd served them walked them to the door of the restaurant and, before saying goodby, cautioned them to take extra care on the road. Revived by the break from driving and the food, the friends continued on. The storm was lessening with every minute that they drove and, by the time they reached Chugwater, Wyoming, it had lifted, much to their relief.

Their return to Wyoming was uneventful, but the unplanned stop in the trip south had been such a pleasant one that, over the next few days, the three spoke of it fondly and often—among themselves and to others. Whenever they mentioned their tasty and inexpensive meal to others, they included an invitation to take the person there sometime because, understandably, all of them wanted to make a return visit.

Less than two weeks later, the enthusiasm for the potential drive and meal built up to a point where it was actually scheduled. The original group of three buddies, plus a few additional friends, traveled back along the highway to the restaurant. The diner had been so easy to find, even during a storm, that they were sure that they'd have no trouble locating it.

Such was not the case. When they reached what they thought were the same geographical coordinates, they found themselves staring at an empty field. Not knowing what else to do, they cruised back and forth on the highway for some distance. They could not find the restaurant, no matter how hard they looked.

Finally, out of frustration and hunger, the driver pulled in at a roadside hamburger stand. Somewhat dejected, they ordered burgers to take back to the car. Before driving away, they decided to ask the staff at the fast-food outlet for directions to the restaurant that they'd been seeking. No one at the hamburger stand seemed to know what they were talking about and finally referred their question to the owner—an elderly man who'd lived in the area for many years. The owner listened in amazement to the description offered by the three disappointed diners. There was nothing around that resembled the place that they had described, he assured them. Not any more, anyway. There had been, years ago, but the place had burned to the ground, killing the two waitresses who'd been alone in the restaurant at the time.

Where Has She Gone?

On a crisp October day in 1968, a new restaurant opened for business in the western Montana city of Missoula. Although the business was new, the building certainly wasn't. It had been built as an enormous private home in the 1890s. In order for it to serve as a restaurant, it needed not only to be refurbished, but moved as well. The journey was an arduous and expensive one, requiring that the house be cut into sections before being transported. Once all of the pieces had arrived at the new site, the residence was reassembled and its transformation began.

It did not take long for the resident spirit in the house to make herself known. Most people believed that the ghost was Edith Greenough, a sister of the restaurant owner; their parents had been the original owners of the home. Edith's presence in the old mansion became quite a nuisance to employees when she rearranged place settings at tables that they had just carefully laid out.

Most of the staff tolerated the entity with some compassion because she was evidently such a sad spirit. Manager Daniel Johnson recalled how once a lady customer had heard someone crying in the women's washroom. Concerned, the lady had gone into the room to offer assistance, but there was no one there. Then, even more concerned, she had sought out an employee to explain what she'd heard. The employee had told her about Edith, the resident ghost, and the story had piqued the woman's curiosity. She had rummaged through official records until she found that Edith Greenough—apparently now a ghost—had died thirty years to the day before she had heard the mysterious sobbing.

Johnson's experience with Edith's sobbing was not all second-hand. Late in 1991, as he worked alone in his office, he heard what he described as a "wailing" sound. Initially he dismissed the unnerving noise, but it soon got the best of him and he called out the ghost's name. The crying sound stopped immediately and did not start up again.

Johnson's encounter was a decidedly positive one compared to one reported by former general manager Paula Sheridan in the fall of 1976. She had been in her office visiting with a friend. Eventually, the conversation came around to the notion that the Mansion Restaurant had a ghost. Sheridan's friend was a skeptic and, as a joke, called out for Edith to make herself known if she was present. No sooner were the words out of his mouth than the glass that he'd been holding in his hand, and drinking from, exploded—shattered into tiny fragments. After a dramatic display such as that, it's unlikely that the man remained skeptical.

Sheridan credited Edith with another prank involving glasses, but this time she didn't break any. As Paula Sheridan and the man who was tending bar that night watched, two rows of glasses fell—but not one broke. Seconds later, the restaurant's heavy front door opened on its own.

Once the restaurant closed at night and the staff had left, Edith was free to make herself at home once again. She would often turn the lights back on, just in time for the closing staff to witness the phenomenon as they began to walk away from the building. Another time, a large light fixture began to sway in an arc for no apparent reason. Meanwhile, Sheridan's dog, who was at work with her, began barking madly at something that Sheridan herself couldn't see.

The challenge of working or dining with Edith in Missoula's hundred-year-old Mansion Restaurant came to an end in June 1992, when the place burned to the ground. Poor Edith may now be a homeless soul.

The Key to a Haunting

Nothing has ever been ordinary about the Baldpate Inn, just south of the Rocky Mountain town of Estes Park, Colorado. The inn even came by its name in a highly unusual manner.

In 1917, when the log building was under construction, a writer named Earl Biggers was enjoying the tremendous success of his novel, *Seven Keys to Baldpate*. The story told of seven people who, unbeknownst to one another, had all been given keys to a particular inn. Each of the seven felt a strong need to escape from their everyday lives for a period of time. The plot of the novel revealed not only the reasons that each person needed a temporary getaway but also, because they all arrived there during the same period, the results of their unexpected meeting at the inn.

When Biggers first saw the Rocky Mountain resort, he commented that he had had a building much like that one in mind when he wrote his book. The owners, Ethel and Gordon Mace, immediately christened the place the Baldpate Inn, and knew that they'd have to include some reference to keys in their promotions. Initially, they decided to give out a key to every guest. It didn't take long for that practice to become prohibitively expensive. The Maces decided to adopt a recommendation made by lawyer and social activist Clarence Darrow, that they simply reverse the procedure and ask each guest to leave a key.

As a result, today the Baldpate Inn enjoys the odd honor of having what is apparently the world's largest key collection. The key to Jack Benny's dressing room, the key to Edgar Allen Poe's college dorm (Number 13, of course) and the key to the hotel room where Stephen King wrote *The Shining* are all on display—along with thousands of others—in the "key room."

But an unusual name and lots of keys are not the only qualities that make the Baldpate Inn a unique hostelry. You see, it seems that the Maces, the original owners of the resort, stayed behind after death to watch over the business that they established in life.

Sudden, apparently sourceless, gusts of air are often associated with hauntings and gusts of this kind have certainly been present at the Baldpate Inn, as have phantom sounds, such as knockings and footsteps.

Adjacent to the key room there is a separate area that the current owners use only for storage. There's a fireplace built into one wall, with an old wingback chair and ottoman in front, facing the fire. The image of a gray-haired woman, described as a "grandmotherly" sort, has been seen sitting on the chair, with her feet propped up on the ottoman, reading a Bible. The apparition has been seen only for an instant, before vanishing in front of the witness's eyes. From an examination of family photos, it's clear that the ghost was that of Ethel Mace.

When a visiting psychic reported such a manifestation, the staff were not surprised. The chair was a favorite of Mrs. Mace's and has often been seen rocking, even if no one's been near it.

Although Ethel's image was seen frequently, it is most likely the ghost of her husband, Gordon, who was responsible for many of the petty annoyances around the place. It's evident that his disapproval of both smoking and drinking have survived his death, for he has taken people's drinks and either stolen or smashed their cigarettes.

As of the mid-1980s, the Baldpate Inn is no longer under the Mace family's jurisdiction. Shortly after Ethel and Gordon Mace's granddaughter gave up her interest in the resort, the ghostly happenings at the inn died down. The Maces may have finally gone on to their eternal rest—or they may just be resting so quietly that no one's noticed their presences at the Baldpate Inn for a while.

The Ghost of the St. James

In Cimarron, nestled in the northeast corner of New Mexico, sits a hotel with a long and colorful past. Its history has also left a legacy of ghosts.

The St. James Hotel had been closed for a quarter of a century by the time the current owners, a couple named Pat and Ed Sitzburger, bought and reopened the place in 1985. It wasn't long afterward that they realized that they had bought a haunted building. Paperwork, foodstuffs and small personal items would go missing—with no explanation as to why they had disappeared—only to turn up days later, exactly where they had been left.

Like all traditionally haunted places, the St. James has certain electric lights that will act strangely, but the ghost here carries the prank even further by relighting candles that have been extinguished. He has also been known to become annoyed when people express a disbelief in his existence. A skeptic who scoffed at the possibility of ghosts in general, and this one in particular, was treated to something of a "light show" as first the chandelier, and then the door near where he was standing, began to swing back and forth.

This presence has only actually been seen once, and it was a youngster who made the sighting. A boy hired to do some cleaning was badly scared by an apparition, which he described as having "blond hair, blue eyes and a pock-marked face."

A presence can also be found in one particular room at the hotel. The Sitzburgers believe that, in life, this ghost may have been the hotel's first owner. She usually manifests as a distinctive and appealing, but fleeting, fragrance accompanied by the feeling of a presence, even though the person having the experience is sure that he or she is alone in the room.

The one unpleasant ghost at the St. James Hotel probably has every right to be in a permanently foul mood. Fortunately, he restricts himself to one room, and the owners have solved the problem of potentially distressed guests by no longer renting that room out. It is believed that this disgruntled manifestation is the ghost of a man who, years ago, won the hotel in a card game. When he arrived to claim it, he was murdered, and his soul has resided in that one room ever since.

Initially, the Sitzburgers tried to expunge the spirit. The response was a powerful and threatening-feeling force rushing out of the room. Nevertheless, it was felt that the exorcism was not entirely successful and, ever since, that one room has been set aside for the ghost of the cheated and murdered card player to occupy into eternity.

Cripple Creek

One hundred years ago, the Colorado mining town of Cripple Creek was alive with activity—both good and bad. There were economic booms, there were busts, there were births (both expected and unplanned) and there were deaths (both unexpected and planned). As a result, there was frequent cause to either celebrate or grieve, and the place that most of the Cripple Creek citizens found to do either, or both, was the Palace Hotel. Miners went there to celebrate finding a particularly rich vein of ore and to mourn a missed fortune, to rejoice at a birth and to lament a death. This chaotic history of events has left the hotel well and truly haunted.

The Lays family purchased the hotel in the mid-1970s. Despite their natural skepticism, they by now admit that the information that they received about the Palace when they bought it was correct. There is a ghost in residence.

Robert Lays is even sure that he knows who the ghost is, because he's seen her. It was the middle of the night and Robert was working alone in the lobby area of the hotel when a female apparition with long hair and wearing a long gown clearly appeared to him. When he investigated the history of the hotel, he discovered that a woman named Kitty Chambers and her husband, a Dr. Chambers, owned the hotel in the early 1900s. Kitty died there in 1908.

Not surprisingly, her death-room is the most haunted. Her image has been sighted at the window of Room 3 and phantom footsteps are heard in the hallway nearby. Kitty's a very welcoming ghost, however, for even in death she remembers her duties as an innkeeper and turns down the bedsheets for guests in "her" room.

In common with many phantoms, this one turns electrical lights on and off—even when the hotel is closed for the season and the electricity to the place has been turned off. Kitty also enjoys candlelight and has lit candles in the bar area on several occasions.

Her tricks may be a bit unnerving for the Palace Hotel's owners but, on balance, the Lays are pleased to have her there. She never really bothers anyone and she certainly adds "atmosphere" to the place.

If you're staying at the Palace Hotel in Cripple Creek, and wish to meet other ghosts, you might stroll along to the Fairley-Lampman Building, where "Margaret" is the resident ghost. She is apparently capable of effective communication with the living, for anyone who's ever been in her presence has come away knowing her name. Conversely, people frequently hear their own names being called here when they know that they are alone.

Margaret's been seen in the hallways and on the staircases of the building. She's a pretty young woman whose hair and clothing indicate that she was in her late twenties when she died, probably in the early days of the twentieth century.

In an attempt to determine more about Margaret, some ghost hunters took a Ouija board into the building. They concentrated on the board, while other interested people milled about the room. Ironically, it was that second group, those who were not directly involved with trying to contact the spirits, who were the ones to see phantoms. All of them reported observing a gathering of men in dark clothing talking in a corner of the room.

Although that experiment failed to reveal any additional information about Margaret, many people presume that she was in some way associated with an office on the second floor of the building. People have heard an old-fashioned manual typewriter being operated, when such a thing would not be in the building. The scent of roses frequently infiltrates the air and music has been heard playing somewhere just off in the distance.

It would be interesting to know whether Kitty from the nearby Palace Hotel and Margaret ever get together or whether their great beyonds are entirely separate.

Gone but Not Forgotten

During the summer of 1986, a couple named Porter was driving through Spokane, Washington. They were tired and hungry but, unfortunately, they were also very short of cash. Much to her delight, Mrs. Porter spotted something most welcome—a motel-and-diner combination with a large sign outside reading "Steak and Eggs, $3.85."

Almost giddy with relief and anticipation, Mr. Porter parked the car in the adjacent lot and the couple made their way across it to enjoy a hearty, and inexpensive, meal. As they walked past the sign that had caught Mrs. Porter's eye, they commented that it was evidently a very old advertisement and that their food bill might therefore be higher than they'd originally hoped. That no longer mattered to the Porters. The anticipation of delectable food had wiped away any semblance of control that they'd been maintaining over their appetites.

From the moment that they opened the restaurant door, the Porters' nostrils were assailed by the aroma of good, nourishing food. They settled into a booth and, briefly, looked around. The place looked to be as old as the sign out front, but the place obviously still had a loyal following—it was crowded with diners.

They glanced somewhat disinterestedly through the yellowed, greasy menus that lay on the table at which they'd seated themselves. None of the itemized offerings tempted them away from their intentions of ordering the steak-and-eggs special. A waitress soon arrived at their table to take their order. When the food arrived a few minutes later, it was hot and tasty.

Anxious to get back on the road, the Porters asked for their bill as soon as they'd eaten. Initially, Mr. Porter couldn't believe his eyes. The total charge for both meals was less than $5! A more careful look indicated that they'd been charged the advertised price of $3.85 for one meal but that, in error, the waitress had charged only $0.85 for the second meal.

Wanting to be honest, and feeling that they would have gotten their money's worth even if the total had been twice what it was, Mr. Porter drew the mistake to the waitress' attention. The woman thanked the couple for their honesty and apologized for the inconvenience that she'd caused. Furthermore, she insisted that company policy dictated that if the server made an error, the customer left with a bargain.

Understandably impressed with their experience at the restaurant, the Porters picked up brochures about the motel associated with the diner before heading back to their car and onward to their destination.

Not surprisingly, they frequently described their fortunate experience to friends and acquaintances. One of the people to whom they told the story knew downtown Spokane well but, oddly, could not picture such a motel-diner combination at the location that the Porters described. The couple recalled that the restaurant name—the Chuck Wagon—was emblazoned across the menu. This added piece of information was no help to the man—he'd never heard of it. Puzzled, the trio consulted a Spokane phone book. There was no listing for such a restaurant anywhere, let alone in the heart of the city. Upon further reflection, Mrs. Porter recalled the name printed on the brochure that she'd picked up in the motel office. That name their friend recognized. There certainly was a motel with that name in downtown Spokane, but he was sure that there was no restaurant associated with it, unless it was just a very recent addition.

Mrs. Porter, however, pointed out that such a premise was impossible—the restaurant had been old, not new. Now completely dumbfounded by the seemingly contradictory pieces of information, the confused group decided that this puzzle would have to be checked out further. They phoned the motel and asked if there was a diner attached to it. The reply was both quick and sure, but it succeeded only in confusing the people further, because there was no restaurant there now. Yes, there had been a diner, the Chuck Wagon by name, at that location— but it had burned down some years before the Porters had eaten there.

The Porters' appetites had treated them to an inexpensive journey back through time—in a phantom eatery.

Spirits at the Bar

The Shoshone Bar in the north-central Wyoming town of Lovell is an intriguingly haunted place. The paranormal action in the bar itself, throughout the hotel and even in the restaurant next door could, potentially, put a person off imbibing.

A customer who went into the bar for a drink watched in horror as the five-dollar bill that he had placed on the counter rose from the surface and proceeded to float away from him. When he made his concerns known to the bar's staff, they were not surprised. Spectral activity is common here, because the building is home to at least two ghosts.

After hours, passers-by have called the police to advise them of a person sitting smoking in a chair by a table. The concerns of these responsible citizens have always been investigated immediately, but no one has ever been found either inside the place or outside. The only evidence to substantiate the reports is a chair pulled up to a specific table, on which there stands a dirty ashtray. All other chairs in the place remain the way they were left at closing: upside down on the tables. All other ashtrays are clean and put away.

One day, staff unlocked the place to find a dirty glass on the bar with a few drops of whiskey remaining in it. The place had been spotlessly clean when they'd locked up the night before. The locks were still in place, with no sign that anyone had tampered with them or gotten into the place in any other way.

That specter is presumed to be the ghost of a former owner continuing to enjoy the business that he once ran. The man's spirit usually visits only after hours, although a few customers think that they have seen him. Proprietor Jerry Hayes knew his predecessor when he was alive and so, when he saw a figure in a plaid shirt and knitted cap staring back at him as he went through the routine closing-up procedure one night, there was no question in his mind as to who it was.

When the jukebox in the bar spontaneously begins to play, or the television malfunctions, or lights that were turned off suddenly turn on, the employees wonder whether it's the former owner paying another call or whether, perhaps, it's the ghost of a former customer, Ted Louie.

In the late 1940s, Ted was a regular customer at both the bar and the hotel. He disappeared one day under mysterious circumstances and, although his body has never been found, it's widely assumed that he met an unfortunate end shortly after the last time he was seen alive. At the time, some people even suspected that his remains might turn up during a thorough subterranean search of the area under the bar.

Ted had a distinctive way of dressing, including an ever-present white stetson. A cleaner was once working alone in the wee hours of the night when she was startled to hear a knocking at the door. Afraid to open the door under those circumstances, she simply peered out a window. The sight of a man in Ted Louie's trademark white stetson did nothing to relieve her fears. She never did answer the knock, but continued working, secure in the thought that the potential intruder was locked out of the building. It's just as well for the woman's composure that she didn't consider the possibility that the man in the stetson might have been a ghost and therefore not likely to respect a locked door.

Perhaps one day the ghostly former owner and the ghostly former customer of the Shoshone Bar will meet in the hereafter to enjoy a drink together. For now it seems that at this inn there's more than one kind of spirit available.

Chapter

GHOSTS
IN PUBLIC

Haunted high-security government establishments are provocative to everyone. To the authorities, such venues represent a substantial public-relations challenge; for ghost hunters, they are a considerable research challenge. Despite these opposing interests, some instances in the annals of ghostly lore are so intriguing that they simply cannot be ignored just because they are officially denied.

When hundreds of people, over several decades, have witnessed evidence of ghostly presences in a specific area, the reports of those experiences are extremely difficult to dismiss. When those same encounters have taken place at a security-sensitive installation, they are also extremely difficult to verify.

Ghosts also inhabit other public facilities such as libraries, hospitals and jails, as the following stories reveal.

Ghostly Air Force Brats

Warren Air Force Base, near Cheyenne, Wyoming, is an excellent example of just such a situation. A base was first established here in 1867—to protect railway workers from raids by Native Americans—and, although the name and function of the facility have changed over the years, the ghost stories associated with the place have remained to unsettle even the most skeptical. Encounters have taken place both inside and outside the buildings. Sometimes the phantoms are clearly that—phantoms—appearing as a mist or haze, but distinguishable enough that the security guards observing the phenomena are able to describe the images that they've seen in some detail— enough detail to recognize uniforms of a style issued a century before. But the visions at Warren Air Force Base are not all of long-dead soldiers. Civilian men, women and even children and animals from beyond the veil are seen—and even heard.

Some of the apparitions have appeared so solid and lifelike that people have actually spoken to them, thinking that they were communicating with a living entity.

Two of the ghosts, one man and one woman, are poignant souls who each died as a direct result of love affairs gone bad. The woman killed herself in 1890, after being jilted by the soldier whom she loved. Her image is seen wandering through a base-supplied house. In another incident, a man died jumping from his lover's bedroom window when her husband returned home unexpectedly. His specter is seen still poring over paper- work at what was once his office on the base. Not surprisingly, the electric lights in that building go on and off when no one is near the switches.

Two Native ghosts also haunt the place. One of those spirits manifests itself only as the sounds of a terrified woman's screams. They are said to be so disturbing that anyone hearing the heart-wrenching sobs tries to find their source in order to offer aid. No one is never able to, of course, for the cries are mere echoes, scars on the auditory landscape, at a spot where the terrible sound originated—many, many years ago. As well, a Native brave, in full war regalia, is seen at what is now a missile site. He and his horse charge across the panorama at a full gallop, off into eternity.

The phantom brave's horse is not the only ghostly animal at the base. The ghosts of a dog and a cat haunt the buildings that they were associated with in life. Interestingly, the base's highly trained security dogs refuse to enter certain haunted buildings.

One of the strangest hauntings on the base occurred in a staff house during 1986. Initially, food would go missing from the house, but the occupants didn't recognize this annoying occurrence as being a sign of anything from the realm of the supernatural. It wasn't until the woman who lived in the house began to see apparitions that she knew that she was living in a *very* haunted house. Her first ghostly sighting was of a man standing at her bedroom door. Seconds after he appeared, he disappeared. The next night, the same image reappeared, but this time he was accompanied by a woman. The images were so real that the resident threw her pillow at them. The apparitions vanished immediately.

Understandably concerned, the tenant asked a friend to spend the night. As he slept, stretched out on the couch, an invisible hand grasped him by his ankles and pulled him down to the floor. This unnerving stunt may or may not have been perpetrated by the same spirits that had been seen at the lady's bedroom door. No one can say for sure, because no spirits were actually seen that night. The next night, however, the ghostly couple returned, now with a child in tow. Although the image of the child simply stood and stared, the tenant also reported hearing a baby screaming. Terrified for the safety of her own child, she ran to the nursery. Approaching panic, she struggled to turn the door handle but—at first, anyway—it wouldn't budge. When she finally did get the door open, she could hardly believe what she saw inside. The area that she'd left neat and tidy not long before was now in complete disarray. Thankfully, her child was unharmed.

In an attempt to understand her newly imposed living conditions, the woman investigated the history of her house. She discovered that its previous occupants, a man, a woman and a child, had been killed in a car accident. The images that she had been seeing at night exactly matched the descriptions of that tragedy-stricken little family. However, once the ghosts' identity had been established in the woman's mind, they were never seen again.

Another house on the base was also very haunted for only a short period of time. No images were ever seen, but down-to-earth folks stood and watched in utter amazement as kitchen drawers and cabinet doors flew open and closed while the doorbell chimed repeatedly, even though no one was near them.

Hospitals are often haunted and the one on Warren Air Force Base is no exception. One specter is first seen as a transparent haze or cloud but, seconds later, the vision will solidify into a little girl's image. Moments later, she vanishes. So does the image of a man in another building. He sits propped up on a garbage can beside a soft-drink machine. His image is so real-looking that people often speak to him and are surprised when he doesn't reply. Of course, those same people are even more surprised when he vaporizes before their eyes.

Like hospitals, jails are also often haunted. The jail on the base is probably home to more than one ghost. In the wee hours of the night, doors are heard to open and close in areas where no one could possibly be walking around. Those sounds are always accompanied by phantom footfalls that follow a predictable path to a back door, which has actually been witnessed opening and then closing again, as though someone had gone through the doorway—although no image was ever seen.

If there is only one ghost in the jail, it's likely not the spirit of a prisoner, for the presence likes to play games with the prisoners by removing their shoes from their locked cells as they sleep. This ghost has decided preferences and has been known to rearrange the furniture in a television lounge, clearly preferring that a particular chair should be kept in a particular spot. If that chair is moved, a cold draft of air rushes into the room. When the ghost's favorite chair is left alone, the seat cushion can at times be seen being depressed, as though an invisible someone was sitting down on it. Often, moments later, if the television is on, it will mysteriously change channels.

Ghosts' attraction to things electric and electronic, such as the television in the jail lounge, is well documented, and so it's no surprise that elevators in some of the base buildings often operate independently of either human or mechanical control.

Perhaps the oldest ghost story here dates back to the late 1870s, when a family here at the D.A. Russell Base, as it was then known, arranged for a piano to be shipped to them from Europe. The instrument arrived unharmed—but possibly with a spirit for, although it was not a player piano, it was often heard playing when no one was near it. That piano's subsequent whereabouts have long been lost to history, but a sentry from approximately that same era has been spotted by guards of today.

The most poignant presence at Warren Air Force Base is that of a woman who wears a black veil. She routinely visits the gravesites in the old cemetery. Her identity is unknown and she vanishes when approached.

With this many ghost stories from one location, it's no wonder that, security aside, the ghosts at the Warren Air Force Base are a badly kept secret.

Historically Haunted

Fort Laramie National Historic Site is thought to be the most haunted area in Wyoming. Originally established as a fur-trading center in 1834, Fort Laramie became an army post shortly afterward. Today, the venue is preserved as a living museum, and the many phantoms left over from the fort's early days add to the area's intrigue. Some of the resident spirits haunt the place intermittently only, whereas others are constant presences.

Legend has it that a ghost known as "the Lady in Green" appears at Fort Laramie every seven years. Her image is as enduring as it is puzzling. The phantom has been named for the old-fashioned green-colored riding-habit that she wears as she sits side-saddle on her galloping black horse. Her image is so lifelike that people who see her are convinced that she is a flesh-and-blood human being.

Many witnesses report that they have ridden out to speak to the rider, only to have the image vaporize before their eyes. Once they recover from their confusion, they often note that, although their own horses leave hoof-marks on the earth, the ghostly woman's animal left no such tracks.

A young lieutenant with the surname Allison made just such a sighting years ago and reported that his well-trained dog, who was accompanying him when he saw the phantom horse and rider, began acting as though it was being threatened in some way.

It is believed that, in life, the Lady in Green was the daughter of one of Fort Laramie's first administrators. She was a skilled rider who frequently ignored her father's advice and rode out too far from the fort. One day, she simply didn't return. Search parties were sent out, but the mystery was never solved. The Lady in Green was first sighted not long after the daughter went missing.

The majority of the ghosts at Fort Laramie are not on nearly as rigid a schedule. In the 1980s, Don Warder, a professor from the University of Wyoming, is reported to have heard doors in the buildings slam even though there was no reasonable explanation for them to have done so. About an hour after the racket subsided, a student woke up in a near panic, sure that someone had approached her bed and had actually been close enough that she'd felt the person's hot breath on her face.

On another night, a group staying at the fort noticed what appeared to be a lamp burning in a building's window. As it is a well-known policy that all buildings are to be kept dark after sundown, the surprised witnesses immediately set out to investigate. Before they even got inside, the light that they'd all seen in the window had disappeared, which confused them even more and they continued on their mission. As they approached the place, they were all deeply disturbed by a cold chill that passed by them, but as soon as they set foot inside, their strange feelings disappeared. They searched throughout all the rooms but never found any possible source for the light that they'd seen shining at the window.

In another building, security guards have seen a light coming from a second-floor window not long after they'd gone in and turned all the lights off. When the guards questioned an actress who'd been on the main floor playing the role of an officer's wife, she was not surprised that there had been some additional evidence of paranormal activity. It seems that each time she had reached the part in her script that called for her to apologize for the shabbiness of her home, she had invariably heard shuffling sounds from a room on the floor above her—the room where the patroling security staff had later seen the light.

Occasionally too, the quarters of the security officers will be lit up just moments after the place has been darkened and secured for the night. During the day, a rocking chair in their building sometimes begins rocking and then stops—when no one is near it.

The building that originally housed the army's bachelors' quarters is also well haunted. Even today, people staying in those rooms can hear furniture being scraped across the floor, and once the trap door to the attic defied the law of gravity by flying open when no one was near it.

Two young women, summer employees at the fort, were sitting on the steps of the former bachelors' quarters taking a break from their chores. Happily chatting between themselves, they were startled by a rapping sound on a pane of glass above them. They looked up—straight into an angry-looking man's face. The vision then shouted at them to leave, that their conversation was disrupting the meeting being held inside. As the two women knew for a fact that the building was empty, they fled in terror.

Not all the reports from that same building are so specific. Doug Johnson, a long-time volunteer, insisted that he distinctly felt that some unknown cruelty, perhaps to a child, had once taken place in the building once used as the bachelors' quarters.

At sunrise, the flag at Fort Laramie is still ceremonially raised. A number of years ago, the man performing that function was surprised to hear a sarcastic comment being directed at him from behind. He had assumed that he was alone as he performed his duties but, in response to the voice, he turned his head in the direction of the sound. Much to his surprise, there were two officers standing nearby. As he began to challenge the comment, they vanished.

The ghost of a sixteen-year-old maiden haunts the Fort Laramie Cemetery. This phantom is a particularly poignant and enduring one. The girl died, reportedly of a broken heart, in 1864. She had been equally well liked by her own people, who were Native Americans, and by the Confederate officers at the post. All mourned her death at a large, formal funeral service. The skies, which had been sunny and cloudless, darkened as the ceremony got under way until, by the time the girl's coffin had been lowered into the ground, a terrible storm was raging. To this day, people and animals alike react to an unseen presence when they are near the young woman's grave.

Fort Laramie's many ghosts mean that visitors to the site might get a very real feel for a historical presence.

A Never-ending Battle

As you may recall, there is a theory that purports that ghosts are residual energy—the leftover energy of a once-living being. Some people are apparently more likely to leave such energy traces behind, and therefore to become ghosts, than others are. Factors such as a strong personality, unfinished "earthly" business and horror at the imminence of unexpected death all seem to be indicators of who is likely to return as a specter.

Further to this proposition, ghostly history indicates that extreme trauma can do more than leave behind a spirit or two: it can actually scar the "psychic landscape" of a particular location, leaving it a haunted area. This theory would help to explain the ghostly detritus often associated with battle sites. Hauntings of these sorts are amazingly enduring. In England, for instance, manifestations of Roman soldiers continue to be reported to this day.

The following story is not nearly that old, but it does date to the early summer of 1876 and it certainly supports both of the suppositions just described. This haunted area is probably the most tragic in the Rockies. It is one where thousands of intense and determined people exerted enormous amounts of mental, physical and emotional energy—the ghost-rich site of "Custer's Last Stand" in the southern part of Montana, near Little Bighorn Mountain. The area has been preserved to commemorate the tragedy. There are now scattered buildings on the site, both to cater to visitors and for the use of staff.

(As an aside, despite his obviously intense involvement with the battle, the ghost of General Custer himself has not been seen at Little Bighorn. However, according to a report from 1936, Custer's ghost was both seen and heard in quite a different location. Surprisingly, the sighting took place in Montreal, of all places, in the Canadian province of Quebec. Dr. William Bell, a dentist, was walking with his young son, James, when he came upon a man meeting the exact description of General George Custer. Dr. Bell recalled that the manifestation had seemed distressed and had kept asking if he had "seen the 7th [Cavalry]." Bell had responded that he hadn't. Custer's ghost had looked surprised, for a moment, then vanished.)

The paranormal elements of this story actually began more than a month before the beginning of the famous battle between the American soldiers and the encamped Natives. That is when George Custer's wife, Elizabeth, had a vision of her husband and his soldiers "ascending to meet our Maker." During the same time period, Chief Sitting Bull, whose warriors were preparing to oppose Custer's forces, dreamed of his braves "falling upside down." In both cases, their dreams prophesied impending deaths.

Having begun with those pre-battle supernatural sightings, we can work our way to the present, for the ghosts of the deadly skirmishes continue to be seen, heard, felt and acknowledged on and around the historic battlefield.

Native people living near the battlefield were the first to react to the supernatural elements created by the tragedy. They were convinced that it was not safe to be at the site after dark. It was during the night, they feared, when the spirits of the dead rose— in the form of supernatural lights and indistinct battle cries.

Although there was no doubt considerable spectral activity from the era of that battle onward, it wasn't until 1952, when the Visitors' Center opened, that reports of paranormal encounters began to be recorded in an organized sense. Historian James F. Bowers was employed during the construction of that building and actually lived in it for a time. He reported hearing many unexplainable sounds throughout different parts of the building when he knew that he was alone. These sounds included footsteps walking across the main floor of the locked building and a pounding from behind a locked door, even though no one was there—no one visible, that is.

But Bowers is certainly not the only one to have encountered ghosts at the Little Bighorn Battlefield National Monument. More than one person has heard what sounded like furniture being dragged across a floor when they knew that no one was in that part of the building. Nevertheless, they always checked to see if anything had been moved, but nothing ever seemed to be out of place. Those sounds would be easy to cope with compared to the sounds of children's voices or the phantom screams that are also heard.

In 1956, John and Phyllis Hamer of Grand Rapids, Michigan, included a visit to the battlefield in their autumn vacation itinerary. After looking forward to the opportunity to explore the historic site, they were disappointed to realize that it was simply too cold to walk around outside for very long.

They were heading back to their car to warm up when Phyllis noticed some strange figures a distance from them. She stared uncomprehendingly for a moment before announcing to John that there appeared to be a movie being made just down the hill from where they stood.

John Hamer could hardly believe that actors would be working in these frigid conditions, so he looked more closely. There, before his eyes, were about a dozen men in blue jackets, astride mounts, apparently just waiting. He noted that they looked very poorly: tired, cut and bleeding.

The pair did not know what to make of what they'd seen. There was no other sign of movie-making around them—no cameras, no crew. They looked back to where they'd glimpsed the strange sight and were shocked to find that the men on horseback had vanished.

The Hamers were later told that there was no movie being made at Little Bighorn that day and further, that people intimately familiar with the park didn't consider what they'd seen—ghosts from the deadly ordeal the century before—to be all that unusual. Images like the ones they saw, as well as those of charging warriors on galloping mounts, have often been reported. On some occasions these entities have been accompanied by the sounds of phantom death chants.

In common with many haunted sites, the electric lights in the buildings on the grounds are subject to phantom activity. When Stephen Waring worked there in the mid-1980s, he reported that he'd sometimes find certain lights illuminated, despite knowing for sure that he'd just turned them off and that no one else had been near the building on those occasions. As well, the spirits tinkered with the electrically powered burglar alarm system. Each time such a thing occurred, Waring dutifully checked to see if the prank could have been caused by a human being, but no one was ever nearby at the time. After a few instances like that, Waring decided that he would make a point to never be in the Visitors' Center alone.

A few years after Waring's experiences, an employee named Charles Mulhair was in the basement storage area. As he turned on the lights, he clearly saw an image of a person standing a short distance away. The apparition was so real to Charles that, for a moment, he thought that it was his wife. It wasn't until the image disappeared before his eyes that he realized that it hadn't even been a flesh-and-blood person—let alone his wife—after all.

At least one of the phantoms in the building likes to reach out and touch his or her corporeal counterparts. A woman working as a volunteer at the park felt a gentle hand come to rest reassuringly on her shoulder. Unfortunately for the woman's sense of reassurance and despite the clear sensation of the gentle hand, she couldn't see anyone nearly close enough to have touched her. That ghost may be the same one who grabbed a historian around the ankle as he was making a presentation.

Over the years of collecting ghost stories, I've found that some groups of people are more likely than others to experience a ghost. One of those groups is the maintenance workers operating in haunted buildings. If it initially seems odd that maintenance workers in particular are singled out, a brief consideration of their usual working conditions offers a ready explanation. These people often work alone and frequently at night, when little else is happening in the area being cared for. In addition, the nature of their work is often mundane, freeing their minds to attend to small distractions that someone who has to concentrate on a particular job might miss. Maintenance staff at the Little Bighorn Battlefield National Monument are no exception to this generalization.

Early on a July morning in 1991, Guy Leonard was going about his routine cleaning duties when something caught his eye. Leonard stopped what he was doing and stared in surprise. There, less than fifteen feet (five meters) away, was a man dressed in a light-colored shirt with a cartridge belt slung at an angle across his shoulder and chest. The astonished cleaner knew that the image that he was seeing was not a real person, for not only was he sure that he was locked inside an otherwise empty building but, in addition, the apparition was hazy, not quite solid. Then the manifestation faded until it was no longer visible.

Guy Leonard later reported that he hadn't been frightened by the sight, nor had he been completely surprised. Although he'd never seen a phantom before, he'd certainly heard ghostly sounds throughout the center. Once, some of those sounds came in the form of an echo or a mimic. As employees were setting up to teach a first-aid class, one man asked another whether he was going to take the course. The man answered in the affirmative and the two set about taking care of the job at hand. Moments later, when they were the only two in the room and were both working silently, they clearly heard the first man's question repeated. Because a tourist had died in that room of a heart attack, the two men wondered if the ghost was encouraging people to keep their life-saving skills up to date.

The Stone House, built in 1894 as a home for the National Cemetery's caretaker, stands near the Visitors' Center and it is a very haunted house. It is so haunted that many people believe that the Stone House is actually the center of the area's paranormal activity. This premise would not be unreasonable, since the place has been used as a temporary morgue for the enormous graveyard that is the final resting place of thousands of soldiers. Some graves date back to frontier days, while others are as recent as the Vietnam War era.

Many of the usual signs that a building is haunted are evident in the Stone House. Electric lights, for instance, behave in most unpredictable ways. The lights are often seen shining brightly after all the switches have been turned off and the residence is empty and locked up for the night. Occasionally when staff members see the lights turned on, they will unlock the building and go inside, thinking that someone mistakenly forgot to turn the lights off when they left. Unfortunately, those well-intentioned souls might as well have saved themselves the trouble because, not long after their trip into the Stone House, they've found the place once again lit up.

In winter, ample proof exists that no living being is responsible for turning on the lights: they've often been seen to glow at unexpected times—even though there are no footsteps in the snow leading to or from the Stone House.

At twilight on one spring day in 1980, a Native historian named Mardell Plainfeather and her young daughter noted that the second floor of the Stone House was alight. Because of all the strange tales that she'd heard surrounding the haunted house, Mardell went to a residence on the site. She explained to the couple who lived there what she'd seen and that she thought someone should go in and turn the lights off, but that she hesitated to go into the house by herself. Mike Massie and his wife, Ruth, both understood Mardell's feelings and Mike immediately agreed to go into the Stone House with her. Ruth stayed behind and continued watching television in the Massies' staff quarters.

Oddly, Mardell and Mike's mission was accomplished without incident and it was Ruth who had the fright. Mardell and Mike checked the first floor of the house thoroughly and found everything to be normal. On the second floor they found no one, so they simply turned off the lights and headed back to the Massies' suite. They found Ruth Massie standing at the front door looking extremely distraught. The television that Ruth had been watching suddenly broadcast a voice that enunciated only two words—"second floor." The incident left the trio under-standably shaken.

That supernatural experience was not an isolated event for Mardell. She has also seen Native warriors on mounts looking at her from the horizon of the battlefield. The vision gave her a sensation of calmness. She suspects that the phantoms appeared to encourage her to keep telling the Native American side of the battle story.

Several apparitions have been seen in the Stone House, including an image of a woman on the stairs not far from where a doorknob was witnessed to turn mysteriously. No one's been able to determine the identity of that ghost, but many people are sure that a disembodied head seen at a third-floor window is the ghost of Major Edward S. Luce, a man long associated with the battlefield park and who died in the 1960s. As he's never tried to communicate with anyone at the park, it's presumed that he's merely continuing to keep watch over the historic site.

A new employee was in bed and just falling asleep in the Stone House when he felt someone sit down on the bed beside him. The man bolted upright in time to see a partial figure—the torso only—clad in a soldier's uniform. The image moved quickly across the room until it faded from sight. Partial apparitions such as that of Luce's face or the soldier's body are not too unusual in ghost lore. They are thought to be ghostly remains that are no longer strong enough to manifest completely.

Not all the ghosts in the Stone House are of European descent. Native American spirits are also seen. In the early summer of 1982, a man named Dan Martinez was staying at the battlefield site. He woke up to see a Native warrior staring down at him. The long-deceased Native and the very-much-alive Martinez locked eyes for a minute or so before the warrior turned and silently walked from the room.

In the summer of 1983, a park tour guide named Christine Hope had an experience that would be hard to attribute to coincidence. Christine awoke to find an entity in her room. From what she could see of the image and what she knew of the history of the place, she realized that she was looking at the ghost of a soldier. His face made a distinct impression on the young woman, especially his eyes, which she reported looked to be filled with terror. The ghost vanished as suddenly as it had appeared, but that frightened face remained etched in Christine's memory.

The next day, as she and a co-worker walked through the cemetery, she was drawn to a particular grave marker—that of Second Lieutenant Benjamin H. Hodgson. Later, while looking through archival photographs at the Visitors' Center, Christine was shocked to see a familiar face—the face of the frightened-looking ghost who had visited her room. He was identified in the picture as "Second Lieutenant Benjamin H. Hodgson."

Christine is not the only staff member at the park to have seen Hodgson's spirit. Susan Reyes and another worker were driving back to their dormitory one evening when they suddenly noticed a man walking along the middle of the roadway. Startled, they veered off onto the shoulder and immediately stopped their truck and got out to investigate. The man whom they were afraid that they'd hit was not there. They searched the area carefully but found nothing, even though they had both clearly seen a man with a handlebar mustache in a cavalry officer's uniform, limping, as though with an injured leg. They soon realized that they'd seen a ghost. A bit of research led them to believe that the image that they'd seen was that of Second Lieutenant Hodgson. Hodgson's ghost is also frequently seen by the river at the exact spot where the battle-wounded man met his slow and terrifying death after being dragged by his panicked horse.

As the paranormal activity continues in and around the Little Bighorn Battlefield site, it's no wonder that the area's often considered to be the most haunted place in the western states.

Dying to Haunt

There's a ghost in southwest Wyoming who haunts the Fort Bridger Cemetery.

Groundskeeper Ramon Arthur first saw the apparition just weeks after he started working there in May of 1987. He was cutting the grass around the graves when something moving along a nearby row of monuments attracted his attention. Ramon explained that the vision was so close to him that he and it could have reached out and touched each other. The worker described the image's modern-day clothes as ordinary, but added that its cowboy hat was the "whitest" that he'd ever seen. An even more striking feature that Ramon Arthur noticed about the ghost was that it had no discernible facial features.

Once he got over the shock of realizing that he was seeing a ghost, Arthur was very accepting of his paranormal work partner. He didn't always *see* him, however. Occasionally, he'd hear footsteps approaching on the gravel path where he was working. At those times there was nothing to be seen, but Arthur both heard and felt a presence walk toward and then past him.

This cemetery ghost liked to play pranks, such as turning on and off the sprinkler system. But there were fringe benefits. Once, when his riding lawnmower became stuck, Arthur got off it and lifted up one side of the machine to free it. An invisible hand considerately lifted up the other side.

The ghost never seemed to mean any harm to Ramon or to anyone else. His pranks were, at worst, apparently intent only on attention-getting and, at best, attempts at being helpful. The spirit may have been lonely, for it followed Ramon home one day. Further supporting the possibility of loneliness is the fact that the ghost is no longer present in the cemetery—not since June 1988, when a widow died and was buried beside her predeceased husband. Perhaps now, in death, the couple have been reunited and the man with the "whitest" cowboy hat is no longer lonely.

A Spirit in the Stacks

Not all hauntings in or near cemeteries can be credited to those buried there. In Cochrane, Alberta, in the Rocky Mountain foothills, the town's library, located on the site of an old church and graveyard, is very haunted. Archeologists have recently unearthed a coffin containing the remains of a child's body from the site. However, the staff in the library know almost for certain who the spirit is that haunts their bookshelf-lined building—Nan Boothby, the town's former chief librarian.

The ghost can be trying sometimes, but apparently she means no harm. The staff recognize that Nan's tricks are designed only to "get their goat" and they readily admit that her ploys are successful. She apparently knocks books down from shelves and shuffles the cards in the card catalogue at will. Given that the spirit's been at work in the stacks for nearly forty years, it's just as well that the staff have such a positive attitude toward her—it seems that she's there to stay.

Too Close for Comfort

Determining the reasons why some places are homes to ghosts can be a puzzle. Such is not the case in the following story. It is a completely understandable haunting that occurred at a house in the historic Sandy area of Utah, near Salt Lake City. The building has been torn down now and it is to be hoped that the restless spirits that once inhabited it have gone on to their rest.

When the spirits were active, however, they certainly made life difficult for the owners. Doors would slam, cupboards left closed would be found open and, if the television was turned off, it might well come on, apparently on its own. Conversely, if anyone in the family tried to watch a show, the same television was likely to turn off for no apparent reason.

Although the owners kept quiet about their strange living conditions, the house began to develop something of a reputation. City workers refused to enter the premises. Neighborhood children noticed that this one particular house on 90th South was forebodingly different. But, in spite of it all, the family stayed on because, among other things, they loved the location of their home. It was so quiet there—mostly, they believed, because it was right next to a cemetery.

The riddle of this haunted house was not solved until the property was purchased by the city. The authorities needed the land on which the house stood in order to widen a roadway. Before demolishing it, crews dug an excavation around the place and unearthed a chilling artifact—a cross of the type used to mark a grave. It seems that the family home had been built not beside the graveyard, as the family had thought, but rather in it. No wonder the house was haunted!

A Hilltop Haunt

A wonderfully romantic ghost legend lives on in the Hilltop Cemetery in Central City, Colorado. The paranormal activity focuses around the headstone erected to the memory of John Edward Cameron, who died on November 1, 1887, at the tender age of twenty-eight. Although over one hundred years have passed, someone still remembers to honor the anniversary of his death. The manifestation of a beautiful woman dressed in black Victorian-era clothing is seen placing a posy of blue columbines at the man's grave every year on November 1.

So far, the image has eluded all attempts to confront her. When approached, she initially flees and, once a certain distance from the grave, simply vanishes. Because the image has also been seen hovering about the marker on April 5, some people speculate that the ghost is the spirit of John Edward Cameron's fiancée and that April 5 was to have been their wedding day.

Disrupted Souls

More than a century ago in Denver, Colorado, the civic authorities were concerned about two issues. The first was the need for a park in the downtown area. The second was the run-down condition of an old, abandoned paupers' graveyard near the city center. The city's leaders decided that turning the cemetery into a park would solve both problems.

With the intention to accomplish their task and still show respect in death to those who may not have had much dignity accorded them in life, the planners arranged to have the coffins disinterred and moved to a new location. However, for hours after the mass removal was accomplished, groaning sounds were heard throughout the excavated area. People who went to investigate the mournful noises were frightened by the sight of shapes and figures floating all about. Nearby residents who stayed indoors were witness to even more unnerving images:

inside their homes they saw apparitions reflected in mirrors and walking through walls.

Most of the spirits are once again at rest by now, but there are those who say that to this day the park remains haunted by the ghosts of those poor disturbed souls.

Holy Ghosts

In 1966, Reverend Eugene Todd traveled from Wyoming to Colorado to meet with a very elderly man who had asked to talk to him. For the minister, a request for a home visit was not out of the ordinary; it was the distance away from his home parish that made the call remarkable.

After Todd and the man had talked for a while, **both** felt relieved. The elderly man, now confined to a chronic-care institution, had unburdened himself of the terrible secret that he'd held in his soul for most of his life. The minister, for his part, finally had an explanation for at least one of the ghosts in his church.

The tragic tale began in 1886, when the teller of the tale was just a young man. A stonemason by trade, he had recently emigrated from Sweden. He and a countryman were hired to work on the construction of a church tower in Cheyenne, Wyoming. They were proud to be entrusted with the project because the church, St. Mark's Episcopal, was a veritable work of art. It was replacing the original building, the first church erected in the state, which had stood on the site since 1868.

The stonemasons' work progressed well and on schedule until the tower reached a height of forty feet (twelve meters). The next day, only one of the two men showed up for work. Other workers at the site noted that he seemed extremely nervous and did not stay at work for more than a few hours. He left without telling anyone where he was going. He never returned and, until that day in 1966 when he spoke with Reverend Eugene Todd, never offered an explanation to anyone for his strange behavior. It seems that his friend had accidentally fallen to his death. The surviving stonemason, terrified of being accused of murder, simply went off to seek his fortune elsewhere. (What became of the dead body is not known. One might guess that the survivor discreetly buried it.)

With the loss of the artisans working on the tower, that phase of the construction was capped off. As the rest of the crew continued to work on the church, they often complained of hearing strange sounds: hammering noises from an empty corner of the church, a muffled voice from another. These sounds were often accompanied by feelings of a presence where there clearly was no one around. Not surprisingly, the builders finished their work as quickly as they were able to and moved on to other assignments.

The unnerved workers may have left, but the strange sounds continued. In 1927, the decision was made to extend the tower to the sixty-foot (eighteen-meter) height that had originally been planned, before the mysterious disappearance of the two stonemasons. This additional twenty feet (six meters) of construction should have been a straightforward undertaking. It was not. Even though the artisans hired to complete the tower were well qualified and experienced, they ran into one problem after another. Worse, they hated being on this job. Almost to a person, they complained of vague feelings of unease while attempting to carry out their tasks.

The workers decided that the place was haunted and that the only way that the living and the dead could cohabit peacefully would be if the ghost had its own room. They set about creating a separate space for the presence. Unfortunately, their purposes weren't fully accomplished, because ghostly noises and sightings continued to be reported. Nevertheless, the tower was eventually completed.

A newspaper reporter, checking on the story of the haunting, visited the church and saw what he presumed was a parishioner, sitting in one of the pews. Not wanting to startle anybody, he approached the seated person hesitantly. Just as he felt that he was close enough to speak, the image simply vanished.

More recently, a psychic was contracted by a local radio station to tour the building with some station personnel and report, on air, what she found. The woman sensed far more than just the soul of the long-dead stonemason. She also identified the spirit of George Rafter, St. Mark's first minister, and the spirits of many children who, over the years, had been responsible for the ringing of the church bells. Ghost lights in the form of both blue and white balls of energy were also noted.

When a phantom voice warned the group in the church to "get out while you still have your mind," the psychic pleaded with the spirits to move on. Minutes later, the church bells began to ring madly, yet there was no one near them. We hope that not all the ghosts left during that musical cacophony, for Reverend Todd reported that he took comfort from the spiritual presences in the church.

School Spirits

In haunted schools, it is often the janitorial staff who notice paranormal presences before anyone else does. It probably has nothing to do with the inherent sensitivity of the people performing that particular job but everything to do with them being in the schools during quiet periods. Not only is it usually quiet when they are working, but the students and teachers who occupy the premises during the day are generally very focused. Janitorial work, on the other hand, is most often solitary, bereft of interpersonal interaction. Moreover, the routine nature of many of their tasks provides freedom to allow their attentions to become aware of more subtle messages—such as ones from beyond the grave.

At the Rawlins Middle School in Wyoming, school janitors are apparently convinced that the place is haunted. And from what they report, it sounds as though they're probably right.

A member of the custodial staff was surprised to see lights shining in a room that should've been empty. He went to turn the lights off and was startled to see a woman in the room. She stood there for a moment before fading gradually as she walked away.

On another occasion, when a janitor took his dog to work with him, he was surprised that the normally obedient animal not only refused to go into the school but would not stop barking. This event is interesting in light of the history that animals (and young children) have of being much more aware of other-worldly presences than adults are.

Another cleaner stood and stared in amazement as an apparition of a woman floated up against a classroom window.

At least that experience prepared him for the time he saw the same woman go walking into the gym. Believing that he had the apparition cornered, he immediately followed after it. But, when he looked into the gym, no one was there.

A police officer patroling the neighborhood of the school once caught an ethereal female image in the beam of his flashlight as he looked through a window. When he investigated more closely, he found that the room in which he'd spotted the image was, in fact, locked and empty.

The woman's ghost is not the only one at the Rawlins school. A neatly attired male apparition attempted to communicate in both English and Spanish before a frightened woman realized that the image didn't have a head. The observer was so sure of what she'd seen that she called the police. They searched the premises but couldn't find any trace of the image that she had described.

This school's haunting seems to be past its prime by now. Even the reports of shadowy shapes along the corridors and electrical cleaning equipment acting up have lessened considerably since the late 1980s. Perhaps the spirits' leftover energies have dissipated by now.

As with the school in Rawlins, it is the cleaning staff at Rocky Mountain High School in Byron, Wyoming, who have most been made aware of paranormal presences in that school. When one cleaner made her way to a specific area of the second floor, she was temporarily paralyzed by an isolated ghastly smell. She stood frozen in place and watched a smoky haze of a whirlwind make its way down the corridor away from her. The woman was so convinced that she'd been witness to something supernatural that she refused to return to that part of the school.

The history of the haunting goes back to the 1950s. Some people wonder if the ghost is the spirit of one of Byron's earliest teachers, who was a victim of a natural gas fire in the 1920s. There's no way to verify this speculation, however, until the presence manifests itself in such a way that someone can see what it looks like.

One of the first encounters with the specter was an especially chilling one. A member of the administration staff was alone in the school one evening cleaning up a backlog of paperwork when he was continually disturbed by the sounds of footsteps. Despite several checks in the area he heard the noises coming from, he could not see anything. For a time he tried to concentrate on his work and forget the strange sounds. When he distinctly heard footsteps coming down the hallway and walking right past his open office door, he decided that it was time to leave. Although he'd been staring intently in the direction of the sounds, he'd seen nothing pass his office. Whatever was walking around in the school as he worked there that night was invisible.

The next administrator to have an encounter at least had the comfort of not being alone when he heard the phantom sounds—a series of strange scratching sounds. The incident occurred during an evening when he was at the school with a group of students. Intermittent noises emanating from an isolated part of the school went on for some time. Under the direction of the school official, the students divided themselves into small groups and began a thorough search of the area in such a way that all possible exits would have been blocked. Nothing *visible* was found but, as unexplainable sounds like those that had been heard coming from that specific area before, the students and the administrator were not too surprised.

In the 1980s, a window cleaner working in an office of the school was curious about a repetitive clicking sound that he heard. He stopped his duties long enough to investigate. The sounds were coming from an adding machine—as if it were being operated by invisible fingers—even though it was not plugged into any power source.

Many people associated with the school have heard the sounds of weights clanking together in the weight room. Under some circumstances, those sounds would not be at all surprising. In these cases, however, they certainly were surprising, for no one was in the weight room at those times.

Carroll College in Helena, Montana, has a whole host of scholars "from beyond." Some are apparitions—that is, they have actually been seen—others have just been felt. One bright, sunny summer morning, a woman working in the cafeteria watched in utter shock as an apparition appeared and then disappeared right before her eyes.

The psychic landscape in St. Charles Hall, a building on the Carroll College campus, seems to have been permanently disrupted by a tragic event. For a period of time after a student killed himself there, people reported seeing the scene repeated in ghostly fashion over and over again. Disembodied moaning has also been reported coming from that area.

Not all the ghostly activity at this campus in Helena is negative. Students frequently report being visited by the ghost of a nun who died while she was associated with the school. They say that she's never left the college. She's been seen and heard patroling the halls and would visit one particular room at the same time every night. She also offers comfort to students who are sick. Many have reported feeling a reassuring presence with them as they rested to recover from not feeling well.

St. Albert's Hall, the building that the spirit of the nun haunts, is now the student union building. When two workers were closing up the kitchen one night, they heard footsteps on the floor above them, although they knew for certain that they were the only people in the place. Rather than investigate, they rushed to secure the building and left it as quickly as they could.

A phantom priest is also said to haunt a particular hallway in the same building. The sound of his cane tapping on the floor is often heard as he makes his way from one ghostly destination to another.

Classroom Capers

The University of Montana in Missoula is something of a supernatural campus. The Fine Arts Building is home to a spirit with a rather nasty sense of humor (see "School Stage Specter," p. 232, in Chapter 8). That ghost is certainly not alone at the school, for there's a most mysterious classroom located in a building in the northeast quadrant of the campus.

On a certain day in the mid-1970s, while she was a student there, a young woman whom we shall identify only as "Mary" waited in the hallway outside that room. She would have liked to have gone in, but she was a little early for her own class and she could hear some sort of a discussion taking place inside. As the time for her class approached, classmates joined her but they continued to wait patiently for the other group to leave. Even when it came time for their session to begin, the students hesitated to go in. Mary explained afterward that they could still hear an intense discussion, involving at least a dozen participants, taking place in the room.

The students who were huddled in the hallway became impatient with the inconsiderate group in the room. They opened the classroom door, ready to tell the others that they'd overstayed their allotted time. The moment the door opened, the sounds stopped completely. Mary and her friends stood frozen in the doorway—staring into an empty classroom. Despite the unarguable visual proof that there had not been a group of students talking in the room, there was distinct auditory proof of the opposite.

Initially, nothing was said about the strange experience but, after a while, the people who'd had the disconcerting encounter began to discuss it with others on the campus. In speaking with their fellow students, those who'd overheard the conversation most recently discovered that a lively, even heated, phantom classroom discussion had been conducted off and on in that room for years.

Rankin Hall is another haunted building on the Missoula campus. Here the resident ghost indulges in a popular apparition antic—he or she plays with the lights. Even though this ghost has been able to manifest itself only through the lighting system, it has actually demonstrated quite a personality.

Sometimes the lights will merely come back on just seconds after they've been carefully turned off, but at other times they will dim as though being controlled by a dimmer switch before turning off completely. Because the lights in Rankin Hall are not on any sort of a dimmer system, electricians were called in to examine the wiring. They were unable to find any reason for the lights to either dim or turn on and off, seemingly of their own accord.

In the early fall one year during the mid-1980s, a cleaner named Bob witnessed the paranormally controlled actions of the lights in Rankin Hall. In this instance, he had trouble keeping the lights turned on. Initially, he was not frightened by the unusual circumstances, because he assumed that a co-worker was playing a practical joke on him. As a result, Bob finished his evening's work, though it meant continually turning the lights back on. It wasn't until sometime later that he discovered that the man whom he thought to be responsible for the pranks had spent his evening in another building entirely.

On another evening on the second floor of Rankin Hall, Bob set about tidying a computer room. There wasn't much to do and so, after he straightened some of the classroom chairs, he went down to clean the main floor. As he worked, he became conscious of the sounds of someone moving around on the floor directly above him. Rather than going upstairs to check out the noises, he went outside and called up toward the second-floor classroom windows. When there was no reply, he went back in and listened for the disconcerting sounds. Much to his chagrin, not only were the phantom footsteps still audible, but they were making their way down the stairs toward him.

As Bob stood in startled amazement, the distinct sound of someone walking down the stairs continued—until the footsteps reached the bottom of the staircase. They proceeded toward and then past the distressed cleaner. Although no image was ever visible, the man reported feeling a cold draft and detecting a musky odor as the unseen entity passed directly in front of him. Showing admirable self-control, the cleaner finished the work that had brought him to that area of the campus, although he added that he did leave as soon as possible after completing his duties.

As I noted earlier in this chapter, some people are more likely than others to experience paranormal encounters. Considering the number of ghostly manifestations Bob's been witness to around the University of Montana in Missoula, it's probably a fair presumption that he is one of those who is receptive to whatever signals those from the other world emit.

In a building housing administrative offices, Bob has seen lights inexplicably turn on and off, and he's listened as doors slammed throughout what was presumed to be an empty building. After awhile this racket became so routine that Bob and a number of workmates, some of whom were skeptics, decided to determine once and for all who—or what—was to blame for the sounds. To set up the experiment, they first locked all the interior doors, which were described as being made of solid wood and equipped with deadbolts. Next, they posted guards at the building's exits and waited.

Their patience was not strained. Soon the participants in the experiment began to hear the familiar sounds of doors slamming. Each sentry investigated his or her own section and then they assembled to compare notes on what they'd found. Of all the doors that had been left locked, very few remained that way. Some were merely unlocked and some stood wide open. Worse, no living persons, other than those involved in the ploy, had been seen in the building.

The experiment might have unnerved the humans who set it up, but it apparently did nothing to dissuade the presence responsible for the goings-on, for cleaners working in that building during the evening still sometimes perform their duties to a background of occasional door slamming. They have noted that the noises are most pronounced during the hours immediately on either side of midnight. Understandably, there aren't many skeptics left on the night-time cleaning crew.

One of those converted to a believer was a man named Jack. His first solitary supernatural experience occurred in the administrative section, but it was similar to the one that had frightened Bob so badly in the classroom building. As he stood at the bottom of a set of stairs, he listened to the sounds of footsteps making their way down the staircase.

On another occasion in the same building, Jack was in the basement cleaning the men's washroom. As he worked, he heard someone knock on the door. Without pausing, he simply called out that the door was unlocked and that whoever wished to should come on in. There was no reply. For a moment there was only silence, and then the knocking was repeated. This time he grabbed the door and flung it open. No one was there, there was no sign of anyone in the corridor and there was no place that anyone could have hidden.

Admittedly disturbed about the occurrence, he then propped the door open by jamming a wedge underneath it. Jack's strategy worked only for a moment—then the doorstop flew across the room at him, causing the door to slam with an angry-sounding crack.

Jack, once a skeptic himself, tried confiding his experiences to a co-worker named Jim. His descriptions of his encounters with the paranormal drew little sympathy from Jim, until that man had a similar experience of his own in the extremely haunted basement.

Jim was also cleaning washroom areas, but he was in the women's room when he heard the knocking. Initially he called out that he'd be through with the room in just a few minutes. He received no reply and continued cleaning for a moment until he heard a second knock. Like Jack had done in the men's room, Jim stuck a wedge under the door to prop it open. He was somewhat disconcerted to note there was no one visible in the hall but, as there was little else to do, he continued the last of his chores—filling the soap dispensers. As he glanced up at the mirror above the sink he was working on, he was shocked to see a reflection of a woman looking back at him. He spun around to face the sudden intruder but found that he was alone in the room. Pivoting again to check in the mirror, he saw that the image had vanished.

Jailhouse Haunts

The following short article appeared in the November 5, 1884, edition of the *Calgary Herald*, under the title "A Haunted Cell."

> *There is a cell in the Leadville [Colorado] jail said to be haunted, and prisoners are put into it for special punishment. A superstitious woman was thus nearly frightened out of her wits and has since suffered nervous prostration. She sued the jailer for damages.*

In describing a different, more extensive haunting, in October 1906 the *Butte Miner* ran the following headline: "Is Murderer's Ghost Haunting the Butte County Jail?" It's likely that the answer to their question was not only "yes" at the time, but that the place remained haunted for at least the better part of the twentieth century, because in 1988 the *Montana Standard* ran a similar story. Those two newspaper accounts certainly serve to verify the tenacious aspect of the haunting at the Butte–Silver Bow County Courthouse, as it is now known.

The Butte ghost story began on May 18, 1906, when Miles Fuller was executed for the murder of a prospector. There was never anything more than circumstantial evidence connecting Fuller with the fatal crime, and he went to his death proclaiming his innocence. Perhaps that is why, almost from the moment that the executioner's rope was snapped taut by the condemned man's weight, Fuller has been haunting the courthouse/jail.

Immediately after Fuller was pronounced dead, his body was cut down and workers loaded it onto a makeshift hearse. As soon as they had completed their heavy and unpleasant chore, there was an enormous clap of thunder—the only one to be heard throughout the area all that day.

Once the coffin was interred in the spot assigned to it, other workers began to report seeing Fuller's apparition in and around the courthouse. The room in which the deputy sheriffs lived became one of the manifestation's favorites. As there were artifacts from Fuller's incarceration and hanging kept in that room, it's possible that his ghost was either attracted to them or it may actually have been brought in on one of them. Whichever was the case, the slightly see-through dead man caused more than one deputy to run from the comfort of his quarters.

Manifestations of Fuller's ghost usually originated near the window, as though he'd come in that way. The men who made those first few sightings described the image as being made up of "foggy, dim light." Even if they didn't see it, the men knew when the man's spirit was around by the presence of unexplainable phantom breezes. They also blamed the ghost for pulling their sheets down while they were sleeping.

Deputy Sheriff Tom Mulcahy, who admitted seeing the phantom on several occasions, unintentionally supported the

A jail from the old Wild West. This one is in Bannack, Montana.

wisdom of gun control when he stated in the *Butte Miner*, "I was bewildered and excited the first few times it [the ghost] appeared and I grabbed my gun quick, as a man will when he is excited if he has a gun handy."

Mulcahy also remembered being told of a man who'd tried to sleep in the haunted room but had fled after feeling a hand and then a rope on his neck.

Fuller's spirit was also spotted in the courtyard around the jail. The image was so real to those who saw it that they began to chase him, thinking that they had a flesh-and-blood trespasser. When they didn't catch him, they searched but found nothing, even though, because this was a jailyard, there was no way to get out. Caretaker Henry Woodthorpe, one of the men involved in the search, described the form he'd seen as "an old man with whiskers." On another occasion, Woodthorpe saw the ghost in the basement of the courthouse.

Gene Griffith, one of Woodthorpe's counterparts some eighty years later, has seen the ghost many times. The evening after the article in the *Montana Standard* carried reports about the ghost in the courthouse, Gene saw the image again. By now, for Gene and his co-workers it has become almost routine to hear the sounds of footsteps echoing throughout the building, even when they know that it is empty. They know that when the elevator develops a mind of its own, there's no need to call for repairs. It's only the ghost making his "presence," so to speak, known.

Bill Ayers and Pat Maloughney, who also work in the old building, acknowledge that they've been spooked by the sense that someone was following them—yet they couldn't see anyone.

Miles Fuller's ghost may be an active one but, unless you count wear and tear on several generations of workers' nervous systems, he really has never done any harm. It may be that the spirit is not even aware that the body that once housed it is now deceased.

The Haunted Hospital

Hospitals and museums are two of the most likely public places to be haunted. When one building is somehow a combination of those two institutions, the predictable outcome is a hair-raising ghost story. If you could ever add in a cemetery to the above mix, you'd be sure to have an almost endless supply of hair-raising ghost stories. The following linked tales from Santa Fe, New Mexico, are the result of just such a provocative blending.

Not long after an active-care hospital moved to its new premises, the old building became home to a chronic-care facility and a nearby museum took over some of the basement rooms for artifact storage. The rather gruesome stage for ghost stories was set.

Nurses, who should be well able to readily recognize the sight, smell and feel of blood, were sure that that was the identity of the liquid dripping from a wall in a small basement room. Research into the history of the building revealed that the area had previously housed a very special kind of furnace—a furnace used to incinerate limbs and organs that had been surgically removed in the hospital's operating rooms.

A room on the third floor is haunted by the phantom cries of a dying child. Like the situation in the basement, an investigation into the history of that upstairs room removed any question as to why there would be a negative spirit left behind. Apparently, some years ago a little boy was critically injured in a car accident on Christmas Eve. He died a short time after being admitted—in what is now considered "the haunted room." His dying cries of distress are still heard by staff and patients alike.

The death of another patient caused only a temporary haunting. In the days before she died, a terminally ill woman always used her call-button to summon a nurse at the same time every night. For several days after she died, that alarm continued to be activated at exactly the same time, even though the room was empty. Suspecting that it was the woman's soul calling out to them, the nurses would go to the room and reassure the former patient that she was all right now.

One spirit has even been seen by staff. After hearing disembodied footsteps make their way along a hallway, staff members decided to follow the sounds. The pursuit led them to the kitchen area—where they found only silence. All but one of the adventurers lost the required amount of courage at that point and retreated to the safety of the nursing station. The one who persisted had an experience that she'll not soon forget, for she actually saw the apparition.

The image was clear and animated. It was a woman with long, white hair, whose whole being shuddered as though sobbing. The manifestation reached out to the terrified observer, who ran back to join her more timid companions. That same vision was seen again in the same place, through the window of a locked door, and that time the ghost left behind a most convincing memento of her existence. The morning after that second sighting, an employee opening the kitchen found a single long, white hair on the floor, even though the kitchen had been thoroughly swept and mopped before being securely locked the night before.

The new active-care hospital facility that first occupied the building described above was constructed on land that once served as a jail cemetery. Given this combination, it's not much of a surprise that ghosts are seen here.

A nurse, who finally confessed to having seen a very clear, and equally unnerving, apparition in the hospital corridor, initially chose to keep the information to herself. Considering the supernatural nature of the image that she saw, it wasn't a surprising decision. The incident began when the woman had the uncomfortable feeling that she was not alone when reason told her that she was.

In response to that sensation, she turned to confirm that she was alone. Much to her shock, a very small man stood directly in front of her. He was withdrawing his hand from where she stood, as though aborting an attempt to touch her. The vision was startlingly clear and lasted long enough that she was able to assess its rough-hewn clothing. Then it disappeared—vanished completely.

The badly frightened woman felt cold to the core of her being and tried desperately to put the incident out of her mind. She might have been successful in her attempt if she hadn't seen the phantom again later that same night. As the second sighting was from a distance, the nurse was not so badly shaken by it and was even able to summon up the courage to move toward the ghost. When she approached the image, she saw that the little man was no longer alone. He was standing with a woman. This second phantom was equally clear and just a bit taller than the man.

Before the woman had a chance to react to the strange images before her eyes, the female apparition began to move quickly along the hall toward where the nurse stood. The tiny man followed as though in pursuit. She only had time to note that the female image had no feet but was moving along just above the ground. The phantom pair rounded a corner and disappeared from sight.

There have never been any further reported appearances of the unusual ghostly couple nor has anyone ever been able to figure out who they might have been when they were alive, what their connection with the area might have been or even their obvious connection to each other. The staff at the hospital are probably very glad that these supernatural visitors do not drop in more frequently.

Sister's Spirit Remains

The building at 211 Old Santa Fe Trail in the Rocky Mountain city of Santa Fe, New Mexico, is no longer a school but it is still haunted. The ghost is a kindly presence, generally presumed to be the lingering spirit of a teaching nun, Sister George.

For many years, Sister George and other members of the Sisters of Loretto ran a school for mentally and physically disadvantaged youngsters. Around 1970, the school was closed, the property was purchased by private industry and most of the schoolhouse was torn down. Although the building's no longer there for Sister George, she's chosen to spend her eternity at its location.

Right from the start, businesses that located at the site of the school became aware of Sister George's comings and goings.

An employee of a copying service occupying the space routinely heard phantom footsteps and once listened to an enchanting ghostly solo choral performance. He also watched as electric lights switched on and off when no one was near them. As well, Sister often rearranged his paper supplies and even made his office machines operate—all by her invisible hand.

The nun's generosity evidently did not die with her physical body, for the staff of another business at the same address had the good fortune to always find an extra ten-dollar bill in the cash register when they opened for business during their first week of operation.

Although the devoted teacher's manifestation has never been seen, her remaining essence is so strong that even customers who are in the building only a short time occasionally detect the essence of the long-deceased nun. It would seem that Sister George's kindly spirit is not yet ready to rest.

A Specter
at the Station

In 1910, the Denver and Rio Grande Railroad constructed a train station in Salt Lake City, Utah. Although it's no longer used as a depot, the spirits of some of those who passed through the building in those early days have never left. The building's

The haunting in this building, which now houses the Utah State Historical Society, dates back to the days when it was a train depot.

haunted status has been a well accepted part of local history for at least sixty years.

As with most railroad stations, this one had space devoted to a small restaurant or cafe. The main part of the building now houses the Utah State Historical Society rather than a train depot, but the premises still has a functioning restaurant. A worker cleaning up the cafe after business hours was startled when the electric lights went out, and he was more shocked still to hear a voice ordering him to leave the premises immediately. It wasn't reported whether the voice was that of a male or of a female, but the bossy phantom might well have been the same image seen in the hallway just outside restaurant. She has striking red hair and is frequently seen hovering between the ladies' room and the cafe.

Workers have told of hearing the sounds of singing coming from that area. It is difficult to be sure whether the singer might have been the ghost with the beautiful hair or perhaps that of the brunette who was killed dashing across the train tracks in search of her cherished engagement ring. Legend has it that, in the heat of a passionate argument, the woman's fiancé threw her engagement ring from the platform just seconds before a locomotive rumbled into the station. Without looking or thinking, the woman dashed after the token of love—and headlong into the oncoming train. She died instantly and her presence has remained in the area ever since.

Phantom footsteps have been routinely heard at the same time every night. A concerned security guard positioned himself so that he would be able to see the area the sounds were coming from at the time he usually heard them. Right on cue, the footsteps began. Although he couldn't see anyone or anything, the man was terrified as he listened to the steps coming closer and closer to him. Seconds later, he felt a presence pass him before the sounds receded and eventually made their way down a nearby staircase.

The most amazing paranormal presence in the building is not just one ghost but a gathering of them. You see, the basement of the old train station is haunted by a paranormal party. A maintenance worker was called to the building after hours to investigate a report that people had noted lights going on and off when they presumed that the place should have been empty. Assuming that there was a fault in the electrical panel, the man made his way downstairs to check it out.

Once there, he could hardly believe his eyes—apparently a group of people was partying. However, the phantom festivities ground to a halt as the paranormal participants became aware that they were being observed. Seconds later they simply vanished.

A Sensitive Timepiece

Not all artifacts are stored in museums. The Verba family of Denver, Colorado, once possessed an amazingly sensitive heirloom. Their ornate mantel clock stopped working only three times in all the years that they owned it. Those incidents corresponded, to the second, with deaths in the family.

Perhaps spooked by the strange timepiece, Helen Verba decided to get rid of the apparently haunted clock. She took it to an antique store and asked the shop owner to sell it for her. Whatever spirit was embodied by the clock, it was clearly not pleased to have been sent away, for the next time the store's personnel looked at it, the face of the clock had turned upside down. Sadly, there is no record today of what's happened to that particular object. Next time you wander into an antique store, there's a ghost of a chance that you might happen upon that very clock.

Chapter 8

STAGE FRIGHT

Whether it's the superstitions around performing, the thrill of playing to a packed house, the pride of ownership, the stress of getting the show started on time—or all of these factors—whatever the reason, theaters and opera houses are prime candidates for hauntings.

Phantoms in Opera Houses

The year—1879. The place—Leadville, Colorado, roughly 110 miles (180 kilometers) south and west of the then-growing metropolis of Denver. Leadville's *raison d'être* was mining. Abundant veins of silver formed criss-cross patterns under the ground surrounding this Wild West town.

Horace A.W. Tabor was one of Leadville's leading citizens, having established a profitable business mining the miners. You see, Horace was not only a miner himself, but also a retailer in this boom town where every resident was a recent arrival who needed to purchase the goods necessary to establish himself or herself as quickly as possible. Without either the time or the facilities for comparison shopping, retail prices were high and non-negotiable. With the profits from his business, and the wise investments made with those profits, Tabor soon became a very wealthy man.

Unlike the majority of the Leadville residents, material wealth was not enough for Horace. He missed the entertainment and refinement that he had enjoyed before making his way west. Returning east to an established cultural hot spot was not an option and so the newly rich man was left with no choice but to import culture to his new home town.

In addition to a general dearth of refinement in western boom towns, another typical deficiency was a general lack of regard for law and order, and Leadville, Colorado, was no exception in that category. So it was that hundreds of people, mostly men, gathered together on a chilly night late in November 1879 to observe two important events: The first was the double hanging of a pair of claim jumpers. The second, following almost immediately, was the opening of the lavish Tabor Opera House.

As the audience sat in the three-story brick-and-stone theater building, surrounded by opulence that most had never seen, Tabor was on his way to enjoying not only increased wealth but equally increased prestige and status in his adopted community. His gamble was a success. Because of the crowds that the house drew, he could pay the performers well. These high rates of pay in turn attracted the biggest names in the business, which, of course, brought in even larger crowds. Soon Tabor was living the high life. He divorced his first wife and, in 1883, at a ceremony attended by the President of the United States, he married the beautiful (and much younger) Elizabeth Bonduel McCourt Doe, known more commonly as "Baby Doe."

Only months later, a monetary crash hit and the bottom fell out of the silver market, taking with it the Tabors' extravagant lifestyle. Horace Tabor never recovered from the devastation and died, a pauper, shortly afterward. All he could leave his once-wealthy and still-beautiful young wife was a piece of speculative advice regarding one mine, the Matchless, that he had been able to hang onto. He urged her never to give up on that particular claim. Apparently the young widow took his dying words to heart for, in the spring of 1935, Baby Doe was found frozen to death in a shack on the mine property where she had been living while suffering—since her husband's death those many years before—from a steadily decreasing level of sanity.

But what of the grand old theater that had once made such an impression on an unsophisticated community? Unfortunately, but inevitably, the building was abandoned and left to deteriorate. Eventually a fraternal order bought the land and building but, shortly afterward, threatened to tear the place down. That threat was enough to galvanize a mother-and-daughter team of preservationists into action.

Evelyn Furman and her mother purchased the Tabor Opera House and immediately began the restoration process. Today, Furman is the owner, operator, historian and tour guide at this antique Leadville landmark. Thanks to her, the stage that hosted some of the best-known names in show business during the nineteenth century is once again home to live performances.

Given the colorful history of the theater, it seemed reasonable to expect that it might be home to a ghost or two, and so I wrote to Miss Furman and asked if there had ever been any "unusual" occurrences in the hall. Kindly taking time out of her hectic routine, the lady replied almost immediately.

"One day, included in the tour, was a middle-aged couple I shall never forget. They were conservative in dress and had a quiet and reserved manner," Furman described. "As usual I led the group of tourists up and down the aisles, through the dressing rooms, on the stage, under the stage, and up in the balcony. I talked to the group when we stopped at each station. All were interested in the history of Leadville, the Opera House and especially the Tabors. I related the history of the Tabors, how they struck it rich in mining and built this famous Opera House—the finest of the time."

Evelyn Furman continued, "The couple I mentioned previously listened intently. As we neared the end of the tour we stood under the balcony near the theater entrance. Everyone crowded close to me not wanting to miss a word of the tour. I continued the story of how I remembered Baby Doe, the second wife of H.A.W. Tabor. She was still living in the old cabin when I arrived in Leadville in 1933.

"As the tourists were departing to the foyer below after the tour the couple came to me and asked if I had ever seen any strange things or ghosts in the Tabor Opera House. I answered, 'No.' The man, in a very serious voice, said, 'I saw a rather heavy-set middle-aged man standing near you while you were talking ... right there under the balcony near [a] pillar. He was dark complected, had a mustache and wore a gold watch and chain.'

"I was astonished and surprised to think they saw this person. I saw no one there beside me. The description fit H.A.W. Tabor perfectly."

Unfortunately, with all the duties that Evelyn Furman has in connection with her labor of love, she was as busy that day as she usually is and so had no time to either let the revelation that she'd just been privy to settle in or to speak further with the obviously sensitive couple. "I had to take the next tour. [They were] waiting." It wasn't until later that the woman had a chance to review the events of the day and wonder, "My goodness! Was it really H.A.W. Tabor?"

Given the history surrounding Tabor, his beloved building and Evelyn Furman, its dedicated present-day caretaker, it shouldn't really be too surprising that his spirit lingers beside her.

Restless Spirits

In Virginia City, Montana, the Opera House is haunted by a presence who can be heard coming and going through the doors and across the floors. It is presumed that it is the ghost of a man because deep-sounding laughter has been heard, at the unlikely hour of three in the morning. There was no one—of flesh and blood, that is—in the part of the building from which the distinctive sound came.

That particular phantom has been with the Opera House for many years and in 1988 another ghost made a one-time appearance on-stage. He was immediately recognized, by those who saw him, as the recently deceased piano player from a nearby saloon.

A Musical Manifestation

The Opera House that once served the tiny Rocky Mountain mining community of Canmore has been moved to a park-like museum in nearby Calgary, Alberta. And the otherwise nondescript building took its ghosts along for visitors to enjoy.

Staff at the park have occasionally been treated to recitals played on the grand piano that occupies a corner of the Opera House stage. Not unusual, you might think, until it is explained that when the melodies were heard there was no one near the piano.

A group of actors was surprised to hear party sounds emanating from the theater. They reported hearing voices from inside the auditorium, the sounds of dishes clattering and the shuffle of many footsteps. When they peered into the darkened seating area, it was as empty as they would have expected it to be had they not heard the sounds.

And there's also an apparition who shows up at certain performances. Those people who have seen him explain that although his image is focused for a while, it is clear that he is not an actual live person. Staff have come to recognize that he prefers musicals. For this reason, and the description of his appearance, they suspect that he may have been a member of the Canmore Band—one hundred years ago.

The Ghost at the Grand

The Grand Street Theater in Helena, Montana, is home to one of the most enduring and benevolent spirits on record. Clara Bicknell Hodgin was the wife of a Unitarian Church minister and died in 1905 at the tender age of thirty-four. She loved children and had been both a classroom teacher and a Sunday school teacher. One of the unique ways that she chose to instill lessons in her students' minds and hearts was to involve them in stage plays.

When the dynamic woman succumbed to a premature death, the congregation demonstrated their grief by having a beautiful stained-glass window commissioned, in her memory, for the church. Some fourteen years later, when the church moved on to another location, the building became a library and the artistic glass memorial was placed in storage. By "coincidence"—more than forty years later—the stained-glass window was discovered, undamaged, just weeks after the Grand Street Theater company had taken over the Unitarian Church building that Clara Bicknell Hodgin had been associated with.

Almost as soon as the combination of theatrical productions, which Clara had so loved, and the congregation's artistic tribute to the woman were together in the former church building, the haunting became an accepted fact in the stately old place. Phantom footsteps are regularly heard echoing throughout the empty building. The sounds routinely follow a specific route, coming in the front door and climbing the stairs before going into the main part of the building. Although staff have become used to the noise patterns by now, during renovations before the theater opened, one construction worker admitted to being badly shaken by hearing someone climb the stairs—stairs that he could plainly see had been temporarily removed from the building.

The worker's nerves would no doubt have been more badly stressed if the entity had made an appearance on those non-existent stairs—she did appear there sometime later, after the stairs had been replaced. The witness reported standing and watching in awe as a light so white that it seemed to be tinged with blue made its way down the stairs. A theater patron also claimed to have seen Clara's image and described a female face superimposed on a haze of light drifting up near the ceiling. More commonly, she manifests herself simply as a feeling of a presence, or in her pranks and movements throughout the building.

Two women who were working alone in an area under the stage were frightened to hear the sounds of someone walking directly above them. Worried that someone had broken into the building, they ran to see if they could catch the intruder. There was no one there. As a matter of fact, there was no one anywhere in the place, nor had there been, for the locks were still securely in place. Despite this strong evidence to the contrary, the two knew that they'd heard someone walking across the stage. They soon concluded that the spirit of Clara Bicknell Hodgin was with them as they worked.

Like most ghosts, the guardian of the Grand enjoys playing with electricity. She causes lights to dim and flicker or come on and go off when there's no physical reason why they should. Once she turned on both the lights and a radio in a work area.

Clara's specter has even demonstrated that her love of a practical joke has survived into the afterlife. When an employee was trying to get organized to leave the theater after a production one night, she was thwarted at every turn. Laden with props that had to be removed, the woman struggled to switch off all the lights. Once she'd left the area, she glanced back only to see that the lights were turned on. Thinking that she hadn't hit the switch firmly enough, she laid down her awkward load, went back into the room and flipped the switch again. No sooner had she picked up the props that she was supposed to be taking with her, than the lights were shining once again. Thinking that a fellow employee was hiding in the theater and playing a trick on her, the woman called out in annoyance that she'd had enough of the joke and was already late to pick up her little boy. In response, she heard a peal of phantom feminine laughter coming from the balcony, the curtain across the stage billowed and the lights that she'd had trouble with earlier came on again. There was no way that anyone—no one of this world, anyway—could have been in all those places at the same time.

The next morning, perhaps hoping to reassure herself that she hadn't been alone with a paranormal being the night before, the woman confronted the person whom she presumed had been behind the series of pranks. The other woman looked completely dumbfounded and assured her colleague that she'd been nowhere near the theater after closing.

It would be interesting to know whether Clara Bicknell Hodgin was a tidy person in life, because her ghost certainly seems to be. Her tidiness can become very annoying to members of the theater's production team. On one occasion, props that had been put out onto the stage because they were needed there were continually removed and put away again. All of this mysterious activity was accompanied by the sounds of floorboards creaking when no one could be seen.

There are few people as superstitious as those involved in the various forms of show business. Almost every theater has what they call a "ghost light"—a special fixture that is left on most of the time to ward off interference by supernatural presences. At the Grand Theater, the ghost light completely fails in that department, as it has been known to glow brightly at times when it is not even plugged in.

Despite the undeniable strength of the haunting at the Grand Street Theater, once people get used to the presence, they are no longer frightened by it. By now, in at least this one spot in Montana's capital city, those interested in stage plays—both the living and the long-deceased—exist harmoniously.

Stage Presence

The haunting in the auditorium at Northwest College in Powell, Wyoming, has so many requisite ghost-story features that it could be described as nearly a classic.

As has been mentioned, randomly occurring pockets of cold air throughout a building can indicate that a ghost is present. Although experiencing such an anomaly would be unnerving under any conditions, it would have been especially so for a certain actor on-stage during an early 1970s production of *The Miracle Worker*. As the man stood on-stage with his hands in front of him and a few inches apart, the air between his palms inexplicably became frigid.

In many theater hauntings, stage lighting has been known to turn on and off as though it had a will of its own—or was responding to some unseen presence. However, as a rather unusual aspect of this haunting, seating plays many roles in the manifestations. For instance, the spring-loaded seats in the auditorium are designed so that the seat portion folds up against the back, out of the way, unless someone sits down on it. The third seat from the left, middle aisle, front row, seems not to operate by this simple principle alone—it has occasionally been seen folded down, as though someone were sitting on it, even though there was no one (visible) anywhere near it.

In another example involving seating, an antique rocking chair being used as a prop began to rock during a dress rehearsal, when no one was near it. Worse, it creaked as it moved rhythmically back and forth, as though under the weight of a body on it. The actors tried their best to disregard this supernatural distraction but gave up when the chair rocked so violently that the shawl hung over the back of it fell off. Once the movement had stopped, a drama student approached the rocker to see if he could find a reason for its bizarre behavior. Not only could he not figure out what had happened, he also couldn't rock the chair. No matter how hard he pushed, he could not get it to move. The chair that had, moments ago, rocked easily back and forth at the command of an invisible presence, now acted as though it were nailed in place.

The spirit on the rocker may have been the same one that a student once saw backstage in the green-room (a place for actors to rest or await their cues to come on-stage). The image was so clear to the young man that he was later able to give a very precise description of the ghost, which merely stood and stared at him. The image was of a woman of average height, with graying hair and wearing a colorful old-fashioned dress.

While that phantom seemed decidedly benign, she was certainly not the presence seen by drama professor Kermit Herd, who was alone in the building and working on-stage when he felt distinctly uncomfortable. Looking up, Herd glimpsed a black cloud of sorts and at the same moment was engulfed with the sensation of being in proximity to complete and total evil. Understandably unnerved, Herd initially tried to keep working through his all-but-overwhelming urge to flee. When he heard a mirthless, malevolent laugh nearby, he could no longer force himself to remain. Herd left hastily, locking the place as he beat a retreat. The next morning, the locks were still in place, and yet the rooms inside had been inexplicably vandalized.

Either the presences at Northwest College are well aware that they are haunting a theater—or a few of the productions performed there have brought spirits along with them. In a particularly dramatic scene from a play by Archibald MacLeish, the script dictates that God and the devil meet. At that very moment in the production, a sourceless icy wind blew down onto some props, knocking them off a table on the stage.

In a less dramatic moment, an artificial tree, one of several on-stage, suddenly lifted straight up from its base—even though it, like all of the prop trees, had been nailed onto the floor.

It seems that the presence in this college auditorium likes to be recognized.

A Dandy Haunting

One building in downtown Albuquerque, New Mexico, once housed a wool warehouse. It is now a venue for dinner theater and is, appropriately, called the Wool Warehouse Theater Restaurant. It is also the home of an exceptionally well-dressed ghost. No one knows who the spirit might have been while he was alive, but since his death he's been seen frequently enough that people have begun to get a feel for his personality.

The man may have been something of a dandy during his life. Whenever he is seen, his image is immaculately attired in a cream-colored double-breasted suit. Because the apparition seems to so thoroughly enjoy the stage-play productions put on at the theater, he may also have been something of a culture-vulture during his life. He's never bothered anyone and, from all reports, it would seem that he's simply content to spend his hereafter near the stage in the theater.

Missoula's Manifestation

The Missoula Children's Theater in Montana is recognized nationally as being among the best of its kind. It is also very haunted. George is a temperamental spirit who can be a real nuisance. When production storyboards suddenly fly across the room, of their own volition, the staff simply presume that George is not partial to that particular play. He's also given people the fright of their lives by making loud noises in an otherwise unoccupied part of the building.

George's manifestations are not always unwelcome. During one performance, the pianist lost track of her place in the sheet music. Just seconds before there would have been an embarrassing lack of accompaniment to the presentation, a disembodied voice whispered the correct page number in the distracted musician's ear.

School Stage Specter

Given that both schools and theaters are frequently haunted, it is not surprising to find that school stages are frequently home to spirits. The University of Montana at Missoula has several ghosts (see "Classroom Capers," p. 203, in Chapter 7) but a particularly mischievous one inhabits the old theater in the Fine Arts Building.

In the mid-1970s, the spirit left a student badly frightened while she waited alone in the building for friends to arrive. The inhospitable ambiance of the place made her feel very alone and decidedly uncomfortable. She was delighted, therefore, when she heard the front door open and, seconds later, felt a cold draft waft into the hallway as the door closed against the chilly night air. Ready to greet one or more of her friends, she hurried to where she could see the door. It was closed, still locked, and there was no one within sight. Before she had time to assess what might have transpired, she heard the door closest to where she'd been waiting open and then close again. Thinking that her companions must have changed their minds and come in that door instead, she rushed back to where she'd been standing earlier. Again, there was no one to be seen. By the time she had made several hurried trips to each of the doors as she repeatedly heard them open, the badly frightened woman decided that she preferred to wait outside in the cold rather than inside, where she would have to bear the brunt of a phantom's annoying sense of humor.

That children are often more sensitive to the presence of a spirit than are adults is certainly clear in the case of the theater at the University of Montana's Missoula campus. When the actors' offspring are brought to the theater during rehearsals, they always sit in the balcony. The seats on the main floor remain empty—except for a solitary phantom that the children have reported observing from their balcony perch overlooking the auditorium. None of the actors on the stage—all of them adults—have seen this ethereal member of the audience.

A Whistling Ghost

In the early days of the twentieth century, Fort Macleod, Alberta, was something of an entertainment capital for the string of coal-mining towns nearby in the Crowsnest Pass. The rough-and-tumble hamlet of Macleod, as it was known then, boasted a strip of four theaters along its Main Street. One of those four, the Empress, is still in operation today, making it the oldest functioning theater in western Canada.

The Empress has a long and colorful history. It has served as a vaudeville house, a concert hall, a lecture hall, an auditorium for concerts and a movie house. Since at least as far back as the 1960s, it has also been home to a very active ghost.

Some parts of the theater are more haunted than others. Actor Bruce Watson reported that while performing there in the mid-1990s he "had a strange feeling [that] someone was standing over my left shoulder down the back stage staircase. I mean, I really felt like there was someone there," he recalled. The sensation, although uncomfortable, couldn't have come as a complete surprise to Watson, for he's also encountered one of the almost certain signs of a ghost—a cold spot—which he described as being located at the front of the house (where the audience sits).

The man's account is in keeping with others, for it is in that same location that many people report feeling a presence and where another actor reported seeing an apparition while he was on-stage. That sighting fit in well with one made by a theater employee who also saw the ghost. Both described a man "with big, hairy arms, wearing a brown shirt."

A little girl who was at the Empress to see a movie had an experience that, no doubt, startled her more than any horror movie she's ever likely to see. The child was standing at the sinks in the women's washroom. She glanced up at the mirror and there, staring at her, was a man's face hanging suspended a little above her eye level. When the child whirled around to confront the intruder, she saw that she was, in fact, alone. Being the solitary occupant of the washroom didn't console her enough to allow for lingering. The child ran to her mother, who then reported the incident to the theater's staff. There was little they could do except to chalk the ordeal up to simply being another sighting of the ghost.

It's not known for sure whether the ghost at the Empress Theatre in Fort Macleod, Alberta, is Ed or Dan. Whoever he is, he is a musical entity.

The only debate surrounding the haunting concerns the identity of the ghost. Some people think that it's the spirit of long-time owner and manager Dan Boyle, who bought the place in 1937. Others, including Diana Segboer of the Empress Theatre Society, think that the ghost is Ed, a former caretaker. Either assumption is reasonable.

Dan owned the theater for many years. He was responsible for many of the functional and decorative upgrades that grace the theater today. With Dan Boyle having devoted so much of his life to the place, it wouldn't be surprising to think that he decided to oversee the theater into eternity.

Ed, the former maintenance person, is an equally convincing candidate—so convincing that Empress employee Bonnie Himsl readily admits that she greets the ghost with a cheery, "Hi, Ed," as she enters the place every morning.

Ed was apparently very dedicated to his job, but he was equally as dedicated to his considerably more profitable sideline of bootlegging. It was that part-time occupation that eventually led to Ed's demise. He was found murdered, and no one was ever brought to justice for the crime. Because the ghost's presence at the Empress is often accompanied by phantom smells of liquor and tobacco, Diana thinks that it's Ed's spirit that haunts the place.

Whoever he is, Dan or Ed, the phantom at the Empress is certainly emotionally attached to the place. During a particularly unsettling time in the theater's recent history, staff members heard crying coming from somewhere in the empty building. "[The ghost] seems to pick up on bad vibrations," the staff acknowledged. He's even demonstrated a clear dislike for someone by pushing an employee down the stairs.

Dan or Ed, or whoever it is, obviously doesn't want to be forgotten. He's knocked on the window of the projection booth and is routinely heard walking about the place. Once the footfalls were heard across an area that had been sprinkled with sawdust. Although there were no prints left, the ghostly strolls have occasionally triggered the theater's security systems.

The most unnerving stunt that the specter's ever played occurred one day as Diana Segboer and a woman named Joyce entered the theater. "Joyce was humming a tune," Segboer recalled. "When she stopped, Ed whistled its ending."

Those attention-getting acts seem in direct contrast to the times that his ghostly behavior appears to be about avoiding human contact. For instance, if people are working on the lower level of the theater, they can hear the entity above them, but when they go upstairs, the sounds seem to come from below them.

For the most part, everyone associated with the theater enjoys that it's haunted but, nevertheless, the ghost can be a nuisance. He can interfere with the sweeping-up process by re-depositing litter on the floor, and he's also been known to make the spring-loaded seats go up and down, seemingly of their own accord.

The ghost demonstrated his social nature by joining some people who were gathered for something of a coffee break in the theater. The group watched in collective amazement as a coffee cup moved around a table on its own. Thinking that either the bottom of the cup or the surface of the table was wet, someone picked it up to wipe any such friction-reducing moisture away. The tactic might have worked, too, except that both the cup and the table were dry. When put back down, the cup continued to move.

In the early 1990s, the manifestation managed to pull off an expensive prank. He was apparently responsible for a banging sound emanating from the hot-water pipes. Because the theater's administrators had no idea that the sounds were being mystically produced, they went to all the trouble and expense of having the offending pipes removed. Unfortunately, even though it was now physically impossible, the sound of pipes banging persisted.

Former Empress employee Trent Moroz gave an especially vivid description of the theater's presence. He observed that on some nights when he was locking up, he could "feel a cold breath from the theater itself."

Only a thoroughly haunted building could evoke such a comment.

Further Reading

Christensen, Jo-Anne. 1995. *Ghost Stories of Saskatchewan*. Toronto: Hounslow Press.

Christensen, Jo-Anne. 1996. *Ghost Stories of British Columbia*. Toronto: Hounslow Press.

DeJauregui, Ruth E. 1988. *Ghost Towns*. London: Bison Books.

Fryer, Harold. 1976. *Ghost Towns of Alberta*. Langley: Stagecoach Publishing.

Fryer, Harold. 1982. *Ghost Towns of Southern Alberta*. Vol. 1. Surrey: Heritage House Publishing Company Ltd.

Martin, MaryJoy. 1985. *Twilight Dwellers: Ghosts, Ghouls & Goblins of Colorado*. Boulder: Pruett Publishing.

Munn, Debra D. 1989. *Ghosts on the Range: Eerie True Tales of Wyoming*. Boulder: Pruett Publishing.

Musson, James. 1995. *Grand Delusions: Henry Hoet and Cobblestone Manor*. Edmonton: Brightest Pebble Publishing Company.

Smith, Barbara. 1993. *Ghost Stories of Alberta*. Toronto: Hounslow Press.

Smith, Barbara. 1996. *More Ghost Stories of Alberta*. Edmonton: Lone Pine Publishing.

Smith, Barbara, 1998. *Ghost Stories of Manitoba*. Edmonton: Lone Pine Publishing.

Smith, Barbara. 1998. *Ontario Ghost Stories*. Edmonton: Lone Pine Publishing.

OTHER GHOST STORIES BY LONE PINE PUBLISHING
More Ghost Stories of Alberta
by Barbara Smith

Cronquist House • Deane House • Hillhurst School
Fort Saskatchewan Jail and more.

$14.95 CDN • $11.95 U.S • 1-55105-083-8 • 5.5" x 8.5" • 232 pp

Ghost Stories of Manitoba
by Barbara Smith

Winnipeg's Walker Theatre • the Virgin Mary at Cross Lake •
Hotel Fort Garry • St. John's Anglican Cathedral and more.

$14.95 CDN • $11.95 U.S • 1-55105-180-X • 5.5" x 8.5" • 240 pp

Ontario Ghost Stories
by Barbara Smith

Dundurn Castle • London's Grand Theatre • Baldoon
Canada's Hockey Hall of Fame • Algonquin Park and more.

$14.95 CDN • $11.95 U.S • 1-55105-203-2 • 5.5" x 8.5" • 240 pp

**Contact your nearest bookseller or order from Lone Pine
Publishing.**

**Canada 1-800-661-9017 • Fax 1-800-424-7173
U.S. 1-800-518-3541 • Fax 1-800-548-1169**

All across the length and breadth of Canada are multitudes of
spine-tingling ghost stories that will have you checking under
your bed, behind your closet door and in your basement. The
tales involve almost any place in the country, from houses and
historic sites, to trains, churches, schools, hospitals and theatres.
Stories range from long-dead relatives returning for a last look at
a loved one, to mysterious flashing lights and crashing noises,
apparitions dating back hundreds of years, unresolved murders,
curses, ghost ships, phantom beasts, buried treasure and more.